WHAT'S WRONG WITH THE LAW?

LORD DEVLIN
MORRIS FINER
ANTHONY LESTER
NORMAN S. MARSH
LESLIE SCARMAN
HARRY STREET
J. R. WARREN EVANS
ANDREW WATSON
MICHAEL ZANDER

What's wrong with the law?

BRITISH BROADCASTING CORPORATION

Published by the
British Broadcasting Corporation
35 Marylebone High Street
London W1M 4AA

SBN 563 08454 5

First published 1970

Printed in England by
The Garden City Press Ltd., Letchworth, Herts.

CONTENTS

PREFACE

This book is the revised and edited version of nine talks in the Third Programme series 'What's Wrong With The Law?', together with the discussion that concluded the series and the investigation into legal education made concurrently but independently by Mr William Plowden. The broad outline of the series was mapped out by the editor with Mr Adrian Johnson of the BBC Talks Department. Contributors were asked to speak to particular themes but were, of course, free to deal with them in whatever way they thought best. Most of the talks were reprinted in *The Listener*. The text in the present volume differs from the original only in so far as some talks have been slightly expanded; substantially they appear as first broadcast.

It was not the purpose of the series to fit the contributions into any artificial, preconceived pattern or scheme. We simply chose topics that we hoped would illustrate some of the most important general issues that face the legal system at the present juncture. We did not try to examine the defects of individual branches of the law such as the Law of Contract or of Landlord and Tenant. We concentrated on themes that affected most branches of the law. In the event it might be said that two general themes turned out to be dominant: that of efficiency and that of justice. The efficiency of the system was the main issue in Sir Leslie Scarman's talk on the law's obscurity and in Mr Norman Marsh's discussion of the law's rigidity. A narrower aspect of the same problem was raised by Professor Harry Street's investigation of whether it is sensible for accident claims, which play so large a part in High Court litigation, to be handled by the courts at all. Mr Morris Finer's talk looked at the legal profession's search for a way to combine professional values and standards with a more efficient and broader service to the general public.

The problem of justice was central to Mr Anthony Lester's consideration of inequality before the law and to Mr Warren Evans's analysis of the inadequacies of the citizen's protection from wrongdoing by civil servants. Dr Andrew Watson's contribution as a psychoanalyst was to highlight the law's inhumanity and Lord Devlin's topic was the question of the extent to which the legal system perpetrates injustice.

Not surprisingly in a series devoted to the system's weaknesses, each speaker pointed to areas of discontent and made suggestions for reform, many of which, it is safe to predict, will sooner or later be implemented. There is little doubt, for instance, that the Law Commission will increasingly improve the condition of the statute book and meet the need for what Sir Leslie Scarman calls well-drawn and comprehensive legislation. New Parliamentary procedures will be developed to take account of the need for more time for major law-reforming legislation. The code will become the basic tool of English law and the statement of general principle will provide a starting point for judicial law-making as important as the precedent is today. An enlarged and strengthened Lord Chancellor's office will very probably emerge as something like a Ministry of Justice, to supervise and control the whole process of law reform and the development of the legal system. Mr Warren Evans's vision of an administrative Bill of Rights to provide the ground rules of fair dealing by civil servants is already near to realisation. So too is the call made by speaker after speaker for an extension of the service provided by lawyers, especially in the poorer areas and to the underprivileged.

This series of talks may itself have helped to spark reform in at least one area, for within a few months of his talk Lord Devlin accepted an invitation to become chairman of a committee of *Justice* to look into his suggestion that radical reforms are needed in the field of civil procedure if the higher courts are to be brought within the financial reach of the ordinary citizen. *Justice* regards this inquiry as one of the most important it has ever undertaken and the leadership of Lord Devlin ensures for its conclusions the attention of the entire legal profession.

The reader will not find that the contributors were wholly in agreement. The documentary by Mr Plowden on legal education canvassed the full range of opinion and introduced Mr Plowden's own question whether the education of lawyers was quite as important to the community as lawyers themselves were inclined to think. In the discussion programme, an important difference of opinion developed between Lord Devlin and Mr Lester as to the proper role of the judge in the creative advance of the law to meet changing circumstances. Lord Devlin took the traditional view that the judge's role is a limited one confined to marginal adjustments; Anthony Lester put the view that the judges could and should exert a more positive constructive role. If the Law Commission's intention that codes should state general principles comes to fruition, the balance of this particular argument will probably tip against the traditionalists. But if this does happen, one cannot but wonder whether those who now call for more judicial creativity will prove to be satisfied with the freer hand given to judges who, at least in the past, have shown themselves profoundly conservative.

The object of this book, however, is not to provide a blueprint or manifesto, nor even to supply the definitive answers. Much more it is to provoke critical thought about practical problems. If it does this, its authors will be well content.

MICHAEL ZANDER

July 1969

INTRODUCTION

MICHAEL ZANDER

From the citizen's point of view what is wrong with the law is what has probably always been wrong with it: it is too complicated and remote, too slow and too expensive.

The cost of the law is notorious. If a claim is for under, say, £30, the costs are relatively so high that most solicitors would advise that it was not worth pursuing the matter at all – at least beyond the stage of a threatening letter.[1] If the claim is larger, the cost may still be too high to make legal action sensible. The simplest High Court action will cost £250–£300 for one side alone and the loser has to pay most of the winner's costs too.

Cases for a substantial amount that one is practically bound to win are normally worth fighting but there is often some element of doubt which makes the outcome of litigation uncertain. The very rich can afford to take the risk and the poor will have all or most of their costs paid by the legal aid scheme. But for the ordinary citizen who is neither rich nor very poor the law courts are prohibitively expensive.

If one does go to law there is a risk of serious delay. In the county courts this is not excessive – one can usually get to trial within five to ten weeks of the issue of proceedings. But High Court litigation is much slower. The Winn Committee on personal injury litigation – the largest single category of High Court cases – said: 'As things now are in this country, delay is a very grave reproach.'[2] A recent study of a sample of over 400 cases of personal injuries showed that the average time for the claim to be completed was fifteen-and-a-half months. The more serious the case (and the greater therefore the need for speedy

[1]See the Consumer Council's survey published in *Focus*, vol. 4, no. 6, July 1969, p. 2.

[2]Report of the Committee on Personal Injuries Litigation, Cmnd. 369/1968, para. 76.

compensation), the greater the delay. Successful cases involving a death averaged a delay of nearly two years and more than two years was far from uncommon.[1]

Criminal cases in this country come on reasonably quickly compared with most other countries. But even here there is no cause for complacency, especially since over 30,000 defendants a year are kept in custody awaiting trial – a total of more than a million man days in prison. Appeals against conviction lead to further delays. The backlog is such that an average appeal to the Court of Appeal Criminal Division now takes over three months to come on.

The complexity of the law is equally a familiar fact. Even the most sophisticated layman is at a loss when faced with the mysteries of the law. Indeed lawyers themselves complain about the obscurity of much of the legislation that pours out from parliament.

But the complexity of the rules themselves is not the worst of it; for the citizen is not ordinarily much affected by the fact that he cannot understand the statutes and precedents that form the raw material of the lawyer's work. His problem is more likely to be ignorance of the very existence of rules that affect him – especially those that give him rights and remedies and therefore require initiative on his part. Through research we are now beginning to appreciate the vast extent of this problem – of how to make legal rights meaningful for people who are too ignorant, too fearful or too lacking in know-how and spirit to manage for themselves.

The citizen's bewilderment in the face of the legal system is likely to be at its most acute if he gets so enmeshed in its toils as actually to appear in court. Here he will probably be amazed by the language, the style and the manner of the proceedings. What the lawyer sees as formal and dignified, the layman is apt to find pompous and often incomprehensible.

But there is more to the defects of the legal system than is likely to meet the untutored layman's eye. The layman gets involved with the law simply through an individual instance;

[1]F. Ison, *The Forensic Lottery*, 1968, Staples Press, p. 179.

he rarely has the opportunity of seeing the system in depth, of evaluating its capacity to develop, or of estimating its efficiency.

The problem of efficiency arises in various ways. On the lowest level there is the fact that the lawyer's image still tends to be associated more with the quill pen and the high stool than with the dictaphone or telex. This is a bit unfair since barristers and solicitors have now caught up with the development of the typewriter and the telephone. The courts themselves, however, still insist to an absurd degree on personal attendance for procedural steps that could perfectly well be done by mail or by phone.

A more serious aspect of efficiency raises the whole question of the reluctance of lawyers to reform their professional rules of etiquette, many of which have been the subject of severe public criticism. The solicitors did not, for instance, take kindly to the Prices and Incomes Board's suggestion in 1968 that they should be allowed to undercut fixed-scale fees.[1] The Bar insists that the public interest demands the retention of a whole battery of restrictive practices, such as the rule that permits a barrister to keep his full fee as soon as the solicitor has delivered his instructions for the trial, even when the case is settled out of court next day, with the result that he does no work at all on the case.[2] Pressure on the profession to review such rules has recently been mounting, especially since the Government in 1967 asked the Monopolies Commission to investigate the restrictive practices of all the professions.

From society's point of view the most serious aspect of the efficiency question is whether the profession is best employed on the work that it now does. We look at one illustration of this issue when we consider whether lawyers should devote so considerable an amount of time to personal injuries claims which could perhaps be handled more quickly and more fairly by

[1]National Board for Prices and Incomes, *Remuneration of Solicitors*, 1968, Cmnd. 3529, para. 49.

[2]By a recent change in the rule, a barrister is now *allowed* to return any part of an unearned fee. But there is still no obligation on him to accept payment only for work actually done.

other means. The same kind of question could be asked about the transfer of property known as conveyancing, which accounts for over half of the income of solicitors.[1] But lawyers have been slow to ask such questions. Life has been reasonably comfortable for most of them with their existing specialities, especially probate and conveyancing, and rival professions such as accountants and the banks have as a result encroached on their preserves. The legal profession's failure to adapt itself to the growth in the community's need for legal services is perhaps best illustrated by the extraordinary fact that its size today is almost precisely the same as it was just before the First World War.

In addition to a certain lack of energy in holding and expanding their position the lawyers, this time in the shape of the judges, have not been as imaginative as they might have been in keeping the law abreast of changing times. English judges are indisputably of the utmost integrity and are probably unrivalled for their skill in handling the disputes of fact that make up the majority of court cases. But when it comes to law-making their record is not so distinguished. There are judges who maintain that a judge does not make, but only declares, the law. One still hears lawyers being rebuked in court with the words: 'Mr So-and-So, we are here to decide what the law is, not what it ought to be.' But courts change or make the law to some extent almost every time they decide a point of law. In the few cases that involve questions of law both sides are generally advised by their lawyers that they have a reasonable chance of winning, and this means that there is normally enough to be said on both sides to give the judge a genuine choice. The way he exercises this choice reflects not only the objective weight of the precedents but also his personal evaluation of the underlying policy issues. In other words, when there is a choice, the question 'What ought the law to be?' is inevitably part of the question 'What is the law?'

Yet English judges tend to deny this element in decision-making. Even when they have a choice they prefer to pretend that the result was dictated by the precedents – which enables

[1]Prices and Incomes Board, *op. cit.*, para. 26.

them to obscure the element of personal choice and therefore of personal responsibility.

In taking a narrow view of their role the judges exemplify a characteristic of English lawyers generally – they see positive virtue in regarding the law as a system that can and indeed should be valued quite apart from its social consequences. Judges emphasise the adage that hard, or hard luck, cases make bad law but seem less concerned that bad law makes hard cases. Both judges and practising lawyers are for the most part content to blame the imperfections of the system on others – notably on the legislature. The few who do take an active part in trying to get improvements are a tiny minority. Even modest proposals for reform are implemented, if at all, only after incredible exertions. Reform too often consists of ineffectual tinkering. The terms of reference of reform bodies are often intentionally drafted in such a way as to prevent them looking at fundamental questions. The Winn Committee, for instance, was precluded by its terms of reference from considering the key question in personal injury litigation, namely, whether it should be taken away from the courts.

The root of the problem of this narrowness of outlook is almost certainly the nature of legal education. England is one of the few civilised countries in the world that does not require lawyers to have a law degree, and a large proportion especially of solicitors either have no degree at all or take a non-law degree. In Scotland by contrast nearly all practising lawyers take a law degree, which is broader in scope than that provided in English Universities. The trouble with the English approach is that practice is inevitably haphazard and solely vocational. It offers no time for reflection or for systematic study of the law and its implications. The result, as Blackstone said, is that: 'If practice be the whole he is ever taught, practice must also be the whole he will ever know.'

Also, unfortunately, the law faculties in the universities have as yet made little progress towards orientating their course sufficiently towards the problems of modern society, and at the same time making them more liberal. At present they tend to get the worst of both worlds – their courses are neither very liberal nor sufficiently relevant to contemporary problems.

All this is not to suggest that the present system is wholly bad. This would be quite wrong, for there is much to admire in it. But despite the legal system's many virtues, there is also plenty in the present situation to give rise to disquiet. During the past three or four years, however, things have slowly been changing. By far the most important development has been the establishment in 1965 of the Law Commissions with responsibility for progressive organisation and supervision of reform of the law both in England and in Scotland. This is without doubt the most important thing to have happened to the legal system since the massive shake-up in the mid-nineteenth century. I am not competent to speak of the situation in Scotland but the English Commission has already won golden opinions for the way it has set about its tremendous job. Before formulating proposals the Commission goes out of its way to consult a broad range of interested parties and tries to study solutions and methods adopted in other countries. One of its most fruitful innovations which one hopes will become standard practice for law reform bodies is the technique of publishing working papers as drafts for discussion by the profession and the public before final decisions are taken. Statutes prepared by the Law Commission will therefore be based on more thorough and broader research than has been previously the case with law reform bodies. It may even use the results of contemporary methods of inquiry, such as social surveys and statistical studies, to find out how the law operates in fact. Lawyers have so far been extremely remiss in largely ignoring the contribution such methods can make to legal research. Reports of law reform bodies quite commonly put forward unsupported assertions as if they were facts; or, through not consulting a statistician or sociologist, a committee fails to investigate questions that are central to the area it is supposed to be investigating. The Widgery Committee[1] on legal aid, for instance, failed even to look at questions such as

[1]Departmental Committee on Legal Aid in Criminal Proceedings, 1966, Cmnd. 2934.

whether legal representation has an impact on the results of cases, or how often legal aid is not granted in cases resulting in imprisonment. It is difficult to believe it would have been content to ignore such obviously fundamental issues if it had had on its staff someone trained to identify and investigate social problems.

Part of the difficulty is that lawyers are not educated in the basic techniques and methodology of social research. It is therefore not surprising that they fail to appreciate the use that can be made of them. Even academic lawyers have mainly preferred to conduct their research in libraries rather than grubbing around for the facts in the field. The Law Commission does not yet have any non-lawyers on its staff, but at least it has now begun to arrange for surveys to be done for it by outside bodies, and one imagines that this trend will develop.

The new spirit has begun to affect the legal profession, which is becoming less inward-looking and is for instance co-operating on an increasing scale with the Law Commission. The impetus to change is assisted by the new phenomenon of the participation of non-lawyers in law reform – the investigation by the Prices and Incomes Board and the Monopolies Commission are notable examples; so is the fact that the chairman of the Royal Commission on Assizes and Quarter Sessions is the redoubtable Lord Beeching. The Lord Chancellor's new committee on legal education should herald long overdue and far-reaching reforms on that extremely vital front.

Although, therefore, the eight talks that follow this one will all concentrate on shortcomings of the system there is reason to be somewhat hopeful for the future. I believe that historians in a hundred years' time may describe a great era of legal reform starting in the mid-1960s, gathering momentum in the early 1970s and flowering in the last quarter of this century. If that prediction should come true, the present new atmosphere of inquiry and of search for ways to improve the system will bear valuable fruit.

NEED THE LAW BE OBSCURE?

Sir Leslie Scarman

ZANDER In choosing the subjects for the talks in this series we have tried to focus on some of the main problems that face the legal system. Inevitably, the choice reflects a personal view; others might have selected different topics. But one issue that would probably appear in anyone's list of defects of the law is the fact that it is so difficult to understand. We know that ignorance of the law is no excuse, yet the terms in which it is formulated are generally too complicated for the ordinary citizen to have any real hope of knowing what the law is. There could be no more appropriate person to speak on this problem than the chairman of the English Law Commission, Sir Leslie Scarman, for the Commission's job of reforming the system consists very largely of finding ways to simplify the law. The 1965 White Paper that proposed the establishment of the English and Scottish Law Commissions gave them the task of recasting the law in a form that is accessible, intelligible and in accordance with modern needs. This involves the clearing away of the accumulated rubble of centuries. It will take many years and will involve the overhaul of law that is obsolete as well as complex. It will probably also entail fundamental changes in the whole manner and style of law-making in this country. Not that the Law Commissions can be expected to do the whole job on their own. The translation of their plans into reality will depend above all on the amount of Parliamentary time that can be made available for law reform. But the Commissions will provide the guide lines, as well as doing much of the spade-work. They have already made an extremely auspicious start. If they continue to live up to the high hopes that are placed in them, much of the credit will be due to Sir Leslie Scarman.

SCARMAN My first question is: Need the law be obscure?

My answer is: No. My second question is: Is the law obscure? And my answer is: Yes. The third question is: Why? And the answer must be: Because through indifference and neglect we as citizens have allowed it to become so. The law is, of course, complicated as well as obscure. But we must not confuse complexity with obscurity. If we lived the simple life in Arcadia, our laws might be simple – though I doubt it. But, of course, we live in a very complex society. We must accept the complications of the law – and the need for a legal profession to master them and to act as our advisers.

But complexity is no excuse for obscurity. The sources of English law are the decisions of the judges, which are collected and published in the law reports, and Acts of Parliament, published officially through the Stationery Office. To these two sources it is now necessary to add the increasing volume of delegated legislation – rules, orders, regulations prepared by Ministers and other official bodies acting under the authority of statute. Each of these three sources of law contributes its own distinctive brand of obscurity to the law.

Let me look first at 'case law', the lawyers' term for the law made by the judges. It is difficult to find. When one has found the cases that matter, their meaning is by no means always clear, even to lawyers. And there is an element of uncertainty, which can make litigation a protracted and expensive business.

To find the case law, one must have access to a law library. Easy enough in London perhaps: but is it so easy for the country solicitor? Then having reached a set of law reports, one needs skill and above all time to use them effectively. The colossal volume of the material available makes for uncertainty and obscurity. There are more than 300,000 reported cases: and some of them can equal the length of a short novel. A recent case which concerned the administration of a trust occupies ninety-three pages of the law report. Another very important modern libel case produced 41,319 words of judgement. It is perhaps not surprising that Dr E. J. Cohn, a very distinguished lawyer, skilled in German as well as in English law, has estimated that a point which a German lawyer would need only twenty minutes to look up would take an English lawyer hours of his time.

Undoubtedly it is the habit of the legal profession – acquired through the traditional processes of legal education – to search for a solution to a legal question in the law reports. Those who have access to a law library, the skill to find their way about the reports, the judgement, or the good fortune, to select the relevant cases – they are the successful lawyers. Their search is intellectually fascinating, their reading a literary pleasure, and their mastery of their raw material likely to prove financially rewarding. But their labours are immense. It is work for the specialist; the ordinary lawyer up and down the country has neither the time nor the resources to do the job effectively, cheaply or swiftly.

When one turns to the statute law – that is, Acts of Parliament and rules made by government departments under the authority of parliament, the picture is worse – although, as I shall argue, it ought to be – and could be made – better. Statute law is, of course, not merely the concern of the English lawyer. The Scots, who have a legal system with a tradition of adherence to principle that differs from the more empirical English common law, feel acutely the deficiencies of the statute law. One is facing, therefore, not an English but a United Kingdom problem. The statutes are elaborate to the point of complexity; detailed to the point of unintelligibility: yet strangely uninformative on matters of principle. It is a pleasure to read a great judgement by a master of the common law, such as Lord Denning. But only true dedication, or the hope of financial reward, can induce a lawyer to read the Land Commission Act 1967; and only specialists can read a Finance Act with any hope of understanding it.

Why is this? After all, statutes are passed into law by our elected representatives in Parliament; statutory rules and orders are the responsibility of Ministers, who are themselves political animals very sensitive to the trends of public opinion. One really would expect them to do better. The truth is that we are, all of us, the victims of our own history and the machine.

Historically – and we have reason to be profoundly grateful – the judges were the guardians of our liberties – and they still are. It was not Parliament but a great judge – Lord Mansfield – who first declared with authority that slavery is an institution abhorrent to English law and therefore incapable of existing on English territory. One of the liberties that judges have jealously guarded is – no taxation save when unambiguously imposed by statute. Governments have been concerned to impose taxation, since they need the revenue. They pass complex and often obscure legislation designed to prevent what they would call tax evasion. Yet this tax evasion is what judges and others prefer to call 'the right to order one's affairs so as to attract the least amount of tax'. I believe that this conflict between two perfectly legitimate interests—the government's need to raise money and the judge's inescapable duty to prevent the unauthorised imposition of tax – is the real reason for the complexity, the almost pathological avoidance by Parliament of any declaration of principle which characterises our statute law. The courts and Parliament are too often in the posture of two men fighting a duel. Parliament asks itself: is this statute sufficiently specific and detailed to prevent the courts from wriggling out of its provisions? But the courts, duty bound to protect the citizen, look for the loophole, the way of escape. This is, of course, a bit of a caricature, but those who practise the law, or take part in the preparation of legislation, will recognise it as a caricature of genuine attitudes, not mere fiction.

I have tried to explain why I believe our law is needlessly obscure. What can be done to put it right? We must go back to the beginning – we must see that the foundations of the law-making process are sound. It surely is the job of Parliament to make laws. The function of the courts is to decide cases. In doing so the courts exercise, to the great advantage of the law, a creative function. For it is not possible to interpret and apply law without at the same time developing it. Nor do I think it desirable for judges to shrink from their creative role.

These reflections lead me to suggest that the solution lies in the reform of the legislative process. If the courts and the profession knew that the statutes would be drafted so as to encourage the courts to look to them for principle and to interpret their specific provisions liberally, in the light of their declared principles, there would indeed be a fresh and clearer climate in English law.

A radical departure from traditional attitudes to the law is needed before one can usefully discuss new techniques for making and amending statute-law. Will the government, Parliament, the courts, the legal profession accept that the source of our law ought to be not cases but well-drawn and comprehensive legislation? If so, will the lawyers be prepared to change the emphasis of legal education from the study of judicial decisions to that of statute law, its preparation, interpretation and application?

But how do we set about securing that legislation is well-drawn and comprehensive? At this moment of the argument it is fashionable to abuse the parliamentary counsel who draft the Bills introduced into parliament. The abuse is wide of the mark. With fantastic skill and a high degree of precision they do what they are instructed to do: that is, draft the legislation the government wants passed into law. Our target should rather be their masters. If politicians believed that votes could be won by a campaign for improving the clarity and accessibility of the law, that at least would be a beginning. But manifestos are not enough. There must be action by all who are concerned in the preparation and passing of Acts of Parliament. I believe the answer lies in the establishment of new machinery of government as well as in reforms of the parliamentary process. We must recognise that most legislation inevitably originates in government departments. At this early formative stage there is a need for scrutiny, to ensure that the proposed legislation in its arrangement and language meets the needs of clarity, comprehensiveness and principle required by the legal system. It is precisely at this point that our machinery is weak.

Yet obscurities need not arise. They can be prevented if there were to be built into the system of government machinery for the rigorous scrutiny of new legislation at its formative stage.

There are two critical periods which call for the exercise of scrutiny. First, when the government is preparing its legislation for submission to Parliament; secondly, when the legislation is passing through Parliament. All European countries and almost all Commonwealth countries have a government department – a Ministry of Justice – one of whose functions is to examine new legislation before it reaches the legislature. France goes even further and submits proposed legislation to an independent body of great prestige, the Conseil d'Etat, before introducing it to its legislature.

What is done in this country? Really vital legislation, for example the annual Finance Bill, is prepared in darkest secrecy. Though on some bills they undertake a measure of consultation, governments regard their legislative programmes as a secret not to be given away. There is no great department of state whose duty it is to assess the quality of legislation as law: that is, to fight the fight for clarity, certainty, and legal principle. The Lord Chancellor's office is too small, and grossly overworked. We do now have the Law Commission, to whom government departments can indeed refer law reform measures for advice. Perhaps the optimist may be forgiven for seeing in this role of the Law Commission the tiny beginnings of the sort of legislative scrutiny exercised by the French Conseil d'Etat. But this in itself is not enough. I suggest that two changes are needed. First, the publication for comment and criticism of bills before they are introduced into Parliament. Secondly, the strengthening of governmental machinery for the examination of the legal quality of bills at their formative stage, that is, before their introduction to Parliament. This could be done by expanding the Lord Chancellor's office and the Law Commission or by creating a Department of Justice.

Once bills are introduced, Parliament should ensure that it has the time and the machinery to scrutinise the arrangement and language as well as the policy of the bill. Here is a task that might well be left to the Lords – where there is a concentration of high legal talent – or to a joint committee of both houses.

But machinery will be of little use if we do not have a clear idea of what sort of statute law is needed. Here are problems worthy of study by all of us. My suggestion is that we start with the axiom that statute law must be both well-drawn and comprehensive. An Act of Parliament should declare a principle, which should govern its specific provisions. It should envisage the making of statutory rules and orders by government departments in line with its principles. It should not shrink from leaving particular applications to the courts to work out, thereby encouraging the courts to accept a vital role in the development of the law. And there surely can be no objection to Acts of Parliament which are designed to codify a whole branch of law, for example the law of contracts or the law of evidence, being accompanied by a commentary authorised by Parliament and intended to help the courts in their task of interpretation and legal development.

If we are prepared to be bold, the law need not be obscure. But its clarification calls for new attitudes from all of us.

IS THERE EQUALITY BEFORE THE LAW?

ANTHONY LESTER

ZANDER There will be some who may be surprised that we have thought it worthwhile to raise the question, 'Is there equality before the law ?' Surely this is something we have long accepted and made part of our legal system ? Even were this so, however, fair dealing in society depends so much on the concept of equality before the law that it is worthwhile looking at the problem – if only to reassure ourselves that all is well. But in fact, of course, even the best legal system could never claim to achieve anything approaching perfect equality. Some inequalities are endemic, the removal of others may require considerable social upheavals. So the question is perhaps not so much, is there equality before the law, but, how much inequality is there, and is there more than we should tolerate ? These are the questions considered by Mr Anthony Lester, a barrister-at-law.

LESTER Many people probably take it for granted that there is equality before the law in this country. After all, everyone, whether British or foreign, has equal access to the courts, and the same remedies, under the same legal system. This is not medieval Britain, where Jews paid special taxes, were tried in a special court, and were compelled to wear yellow badges on their outer garments. This is not seventeenth-century Britain, where African slaves were lawfully bought, sold and mortgaged as mere chattels in the market-place. Nor is it Britain of the eighteenth and early nineteenth centuries, where Catholics, Jews and Dissenters were subjected to legal disabilities because of their beliefs. Today, everyone is equal before the law, whatever his race, colour or creed; and there are no *out*laws – that is, no people outside the law. Everyone is entitled to equal protection, and the judiciary, appointed independently of government, has a duty to apply the law fairly to all, rich and poor, public institutions and private citizens.

These are real qualities in our system of law, and it is right to recall them before asking what is wrong with the law. They have had to be fought for, and there are many parts of the world where they have yet to be won. It is also right to recall that our courts are open to all, and not only, as the cynic might suggest, in the sense that the Ritz Hotel is open equally to the rich and to the poor. Today, thanks to the legal aid and advice scheme, no one need be denied his legal rights because of poverty of means or ignorance of the law for, at least in theory, in case of hardship a lawyer's services will be paid for out of public funds.

In this sense, then, there is equality before law: in the formal sense that the procedures of the law are universally available; in the constitutional sense that the judges are independent and bound to act impartially; and in the economic sense that the State will provide legal aid and advice for impoverished people who need help from the law.

And yet beneath this surface of equality there remains a profound inequality in the actual working of the legal system. One aspect of this inequality is that, although the courts are open to all, some courts tend to cater more for the rich than for the poor. Cases are allocated to the High Court or the County Court according to the amount of money involved. James Mill, in his evidence to a Parliamentary Select Committee, long ago attacked

> the principle of one sort of court for sums of small amount, another sort for sums of higher, the best tribunals for the highest sums, the worst tribunals for the lowest; declaring in fact, that more care is due to prevent wrongs done to the rich than wrongs done to the poor. The opinion which has obtained but too generally appears to me most erroneous, that suits for small sums are suits of the least importance. I think in point of importance, the reverse is the right order.[1]

[1]James Mill's evidence, 29 June 1832, *Parliamentary Papers* (1831–2), Vol. xii, p. 123.

Admittedly, since Mill's day the legal aid scheme and the creation of modern county courts have enormously improved the situation, but Mill's criticism is still relevant. Large claims are tried with the leisurely thoroughness and decorum of the High Court; small claims receive more summary consideration in the county courts. It is an obvious inequality in the legal system, but it is difficult to think of a reform which is practically attainable and which could remove it. The best hope of improvement might be to take the smallest claims away from the courts altogether, and to provide more informal machinery for dealing with them. In a sense, this is what has been achieved in some fields by the creation of welfare tribunals, though, as we shall see later, they contain rather different forms of inequality.

However, the harshest inequalities exist less in the machinery and procedures of the legal system than in the very stuff and substance of the law. Employers and workers, manufacturers and consumers, creditors and debtors, landlords and tenants are treated as equal parties by the courts, but it is the substance of the law which determines their respective rights, not the formal rules of procedure about their status as parties to a dispute; and in substance some parties are less equal than others.

The law of contract embodies many of the real inequalities in the law. It is contract law which governs many of the most important decisions in our lives – about buying a home, or food, or clothing, or a car; about obtaining insurance or credit; or about the terms on which we are employed at work or members of a trade union. Contract law defines the ground-rules for these different transactions. It decides whether a legally binding agreement has been made with the property or finance company, the grocer, the department store, the insurance firm, or the employer. If an agreement has been made, the courts will enforce it. If it is broken, they will provide a legal remedy. But it is the parties who decide the terms of their bargain, though the courts are available where necessary to enforce that bargain. It is therefore a process of *private* law-making backed by the machinery of the law.

The nineteenth-century philosophers who dignified this

freedom of contract with the doctrine of *laissez-faire* assumed not only that people were better able to decide the details of their lives themselves than any judge, politician or civil servant, but also that the proper function of the courts was merely to hold the ring. And, although in this century important restraints have been placed upon freedom of contract by Parliament and the courts, it remains the dominant feature of a great part of the law. The doctrine depends on there being roughly equal bargaining power between the parties to this process of private law-making, which, ideally, will produce a fair result.

In reality, of course, the parties more often than not are starkly unequal in wealth, in education, and in power, and the result of the law's neutrality to both sides may be manifestly unfair. The manufacturer or distributor of goods rarely bargains with the consumer; they do business on the basis of standard terms, excluding liability for any defects in their goods; and the consumer dutifully accepts and pays the price. The employer and trade union do not bargain with the worker about his rights; either he accepts their terms or he goes. Justice stands blindfold, equally indifferent to the identity of either party, and it is the stronger party which is able to tip the scales. In such circumstances, equality before the law is only an illusory equality, and the very neutrality of the law becomes an instrument of inequality, for it defers to the power of the stronger party and enforces his legal rights against the weak.

Occasionally the courts have not merely deferred to the stronger party, but have interpreted the law with an unmistakable bias against the weaker party, even though this was not required by any contract. There was an extreme example in the case of *Horne v. Poland*,[1] which was decided in 1922, and has never been overruled. Harry Horne was born in 1887 in Rumania, where his father was a Hebrew teacher. Mr Horne came to England when he was twelve years old, lived with his parents in London, went to school there, adopted an English name, and married an Englishwoman. But he never became naturalised. Twenty-two years after arriving in this country he

[1]*Horne v. Poland.* [1922] 2 K.B. 364.

took out a burglary insurance policy, under which in due course he claimed five hundred pounds.

It is a rule of insurance law that a person has a duty to disclose all material facts about himself to the insurer at the time when he enters into the contract of insurance, and that, if he fails to do so, he will be unable to enforce the insurance policy in the courts. The underwriters denied liability to Mr Horne on this ground, contending that he had failed to disclose a material fact about himself, namely, his alien origin. Mr Justice Lush decided that on the facts of the case the underwriters were right; Mr Horne's alien origin was material, and, in failing to disclose the fact, he could not recover an indemnity under the policy. The judge declared that

> the risk would vary according to the honesty and good faith of the insured, the methods which he followed and the care he took, his views of duty, the way in which he would regard his social and legal obligations, and other matters. It is impossible to say that matters such as nationality, caste and early domicile cannot be of importance in judging as to the risk that underwriters run in entering into such a contract. To say that is to say that there are no racial differences, no national differences as regards training and education . . . I say nothing, of course, against the national characteristics of the race to which [Mr Horne] . . . belongs; that is not the question.

But that *was* exactly the question, despite the judge's unconvincing disclaimer. Mr Horne had received his secondary education in England, lived here for the whole of his adult life, and made his permanent home here. He had bought an insurance policy in good faith, without apparently being asked to state his national origin. There was not a breath of evidence to suggest any dishonesty or carelessness on Mr Horne's part. He was denied his indemnity because the judge agreed with the underwriters that someone of Rumanian Jewish origin was a higher risk simply because of national or racial 'differences'. The court's decision had almost the same effect as if Parliament had enacted a statute requiring the disclosure of a person's racial, ethnic, or national origins before entering into a contract of insurance. And, sure enough, the leading precedent book for lawyers, following the judge's specific recommendation in Mr Horne's case, proceeded to include in its model proposal form on burglary insurance a question about nationality of origin.[1]

In Mr Horne's case, the court sanctioned an unfair discrimination and so legitimated an inequality in the law itself. But it would be unfair to suggest that the courts always play such a negative role. They have, though admittedly only rarely, declared invalid an act of unfair discrimination against a weaker party. For example, in the recent case of *Nagle v. Feilden*,[2] Miss Nagle, who had been refused a horse-trainer's licence by the Jockey Club solely because she was a woman, sought to invalidate the Club's practice of granting licences only to men. The Court of Appeal decided at a preliminary stage that her case was at least arguable. Lord Denning stated that 'a man' (and by that expression he included a woman)

> has a right to work at his trade or profession without being unjustly excluded from it. He is not to be shut out from it at the whim of those having the governance of it. If they make a rule which enables them to reject his application arbitrarily or capriciously, not reasonably, that rule is bad. It is against public policy.

This is the authentic language of equality. Miss Nagle wanted a horse-trainer's licence, and she could obtain one only from the Jockey Club. In such circumstances, the Club's power had to be exercised reasonably. It would be an arbitrary or capricious exercise of their monopoly power to discriminate solely on the ground of sex. And so here the court actively intervened to remove a consequence of the inequality between the parties. Miss Nagle, unlike the unfortunate Mr Horne, enjoyed real equality before the law.

Miss Nagle's case is not an isolated attempt by the courts to

[1] *Encyclopedia of Forms and Precedents* (3rd ed. 1944), Vol. 7, p. 491.
[2] [1966] 2 Q.B. 633 (C.A.).

redress the balance between unequal parties. In some recent cases they have refused to enforce oppressive clauses hidden in the small print of standard contracts, though they could go still further in that direction. But the judges are inevitably prisoners of their own precedents; there are limits which the most reforming and creative judge could not exceed. For example, even if in Mr Horne's case the court had decided instead that he was entitled to claim under the insurance policy, it could not have provided a remedy if the underwriters had subsequently refused to insure Jews or people of alien origin altogether. The court could not have required them to do business without discrimination on grounds of race, religion, or national origin, for at common law everyone is free to contract or not to contract as he chooses, and there is no legal redress for someone who is refused a contract solely because he belongs to a particular race or religion. The source of the injustice in this case lies not with the judges, but with the traditional neutrality of the common law towards the inequality of the parties – an injustice captured beautifully by William Blake in the phrase 'One Law for the Lion and Ox is oppression'.

Parliament alone is capable of effectively ending the oppression, by turning laws which are at best neutral, and at worst biased in favour of the strong, more in favour of the oppressed. It has taken one important step in this direction by passing the Race Relations Act 1968, which makes it unlawful to discriminate on racial grounds in employment, housing, education and commerce.

The unjust result of Mr Horne's case has therefore been put right for more recent immigrants by the Race Relations Act. But there are many situations in which inequality before the law will persist so long as there is the same law for the lion and the ox. As with race relations, so in other situations, the law should leave far less than at present to *private* law-making. It should govern the content as well as the form of the relationship between the employer and his workers, the commercial company and its customers, the public institution and the citizen.

However, it is not only a matter of reconstructing the framework of the civil law governing unequal relationships between individuals and institutions. The criminal law also reinforces inequality by punishing the anti-social activities of private persons with far greater rigour than it penalises those of large institutions and their servants. The convicted confidence-trickster, or burglar, or vandal, or dangerous driver, expects to be sent to prison; but, in the rare event of prosecution, the manufacturer of dangerous drugs, or adulterated foodstuffs, or unsafe cars, or the industry whose processes pollute the atmosphere and rivers, or the factory which maintains hazardous working conditions, will expect to be fined, and to pass the fine to the consumer through increased prices. While the civil law permits powerful institutions to enforce unfair transactions, the criminal law allows them to exercise their power in ways which it would not tolerate on the part of ordinary people.

It is not my purpose to catalogue a long list of arbitrary or unfair practices which need to be brought within the reach of the law. That is the work of the Law Commission, whose reports will gradually cover the entire body of law reform. Nor do I intend to suggest, of course, that the legal system, by itself, could remove the major inequalities from society; they derive from differences of wealth, education and power. My object is to stress that, at present, the legal system reinforces and legitimates these inequalities. The struggle for equality in the substance of the law is still ahead, and unlike the struggle for procedural equality – the right of equal access to the courts and the removal of legal disabilities – which has already been won, greater equality in the substance of the law cannot be realised so long as major inequalities exist in society. But there could be far greater safeguards than at present against the use of law as an instrument of oppression.

Nor is it sufficient to win reform of the substance of the law, unless the reforming legislation has practical effect for the people whom it is designed to benefit. Equality before the law is not merely a matter of being entitled by Act of Parliament to equal rights, but of being able in practice to enjoy those rights.

Unfortunately, even where the law has already been reformed, there remains a vast gap between what is declared in the statute book and what is in fact enjoyed.

For example, there are few areas of private law-making in which reforming legislation has intervened more in favour of the weaker party than in the relationship between landlord and tenant. Since the passing of the Rent Act of 1965 the landlord's superior bargaining power has been weakened, even destroyed, by the statutory power of the rent officer to determine what constitutes a fair rent for his property. The landlord can no longer evict his tenant without due process of law, and harassment of a tenant is a criminal offence. The substance of the law is weighted in the tenant's favour.

And yet the number of tenants who have applied to the rent officer to fix a fair rent under the Rent Act is far below the number which was anticipated when the Act was passed. In some places applications by landlords have outnumbered those by tenants; in others, unlawful harassment and evictions continue almost unabated. Many different factors are to blame for this dismal situation. The new legislation has had insufficient publicity. A recent study revealed that only half of the residents in eight working-class London streets, in fact protected by the Rent Act, had ever heard of it.[1] The legislation was drafted with grotesque and avoidable technicality. Its complex language concealed traps which only an experienced lawyer could be sure to avoid, and this is the more unfortunate because impoverished tenants cannot obtain a lawyer's services, under the legal aid scheme, for proceedings before a Rent Assessment Committee, or, in the case of a furnished tenancy, before a Rent Tribunal. Legal aid does not cover administrative tribunals. Not surprisingly, landlords are likely to be represented before these bodies about five times as often as their tenants.[2]

[1]Michael Zander, 'The Unused Rent Acts', *New Society*, 12 September 1968.

[2]*Legal Aid and Advice, 17th Annual Report of The Law Society, 1966–67*, Appendix B, p. 72, para 8.

Better drafting of the rent legislation and better publicity for its provisions would improve the present lamentable situation. And the extension of the legal aid scheme to include proceedings before Rent Assessment Committees and Rent Tribunals would enable the tenant, who is normally poorer and less educated than his landlord, to have his case properly presented. The failure of successive governments to extend legal aid to these and other administrative tribunals is, without question, the cause of major injustice to many thousands of people, who are denied legal representation simply because of their poverty, even though their cases concern matters of great importance to them and their families. The extension of legal aid would be an important step towards greater equality in the enjoyment of their legal rights by the least privileged section of the community.

But it would still not be a sufficient step, for it is clear from those situations in which legal aid is already available that many of those who most need advice or representation before the courts, and who would qualify now for legal aid, do not seek it, and as a result may in effect be denied equality before the law. Perhaps they do not know of the existence of the legal aid scheme; or they do not recognise that their problem is one which can be solved with the help of lawyers; or they are deterred by the expensive image of the legal profession from going to a solicitor; or they are unable to visit a solicitor during his office hours without missing work and losing wages; or there is no solicitor within convenient reach in their neighbourhood.

It is precisely in the poorest parts of our great cities, where the need for professional help is greatest, that available legal services are most deficient. Those solicitors who are able to make a living by practising law in poor neighbourhoods are usually overworked and unable to provide a service comparable to that given by the family solicitor to his middle-class clients. Some lawyers, in the best tradition of community service, do give free legal advice, working voluntarily in Citizens' Advice Bureaux, or the handful of Poor Men's Lawyer centres, as they are still called. But despite these efforts there remains a massive unmet need for advice and aid from legally trained people.

The legal problems of the poor are certainly no simpler than those of the well-to-do: problems related to unemployment, social security, family breakdown, council housing, and hire purchase can be as complex as problems about conveyancing, inheritance, taxation, and company affairs. They demand the same skill and dedication from lawyers. And the fact that they do not receive the same attention is no criticism of the lawyers. When the legal aid scheme was devised, it was grafted upon the existing private structure of the legal profession, without altering that structure significantly. Lawyers, like accountants, architects, stockbrokers, and other professions, were not then and are not now well organised to provide a service for the poor. They cannot fairly be blamed therefore if their office location, their forbidding style, their working hours, or their need to make a profit, impair their ability to provide a social service.

But what this does mean is that the legal aid scheme is shaped and restricted by the limits of the legal profession's traditional structure. Those limits will cramp its effectiveness unless the present scheme is supplemented by a new system of urban legal centres, located in areas of special need within the conurbations, and staffed full-time by independent state-salaried lawyers.[1] Such centres could remain open after working hours; they could work closely with local welfare officers; their staff could specialise in the particular problems of the neighbourhood, giving expert advice, and, where necessary, referring cases to private practitioners.

The present legal aid scheme is generous, but, like much of the law itself, it is based upon a concept of neutrality: the lawyer serves rich and poor alike; the well-to-do pay for themselves; the state pays for the impoverished. But, as with the content of the law, there will be no genuine equality before the law unless our legal services discriminate positively in favour of the weak.

[1]See generally *Justice for All*, Fabian Research Pamphlet (No. 273), December 1968.

areas in O in relation to reform,

IS THE LAW TOO RIGID?

NORMAN S. MARSH, Q.C.

ZANDER The problem of rigidity faces all legal systems, for law is by its nature backward-looking. Any system that bases decisions today on what was decided yesterday is bound to have difficulty in keeping itself abreast of changing times. In the case of our system we complicate the problem by having a doctrine of binding precedent which is particularly strict by comparison with that in other countries. The judges do have a certain freedom to develop the law but even strong and creative judges like Lord Devlin and Lord Denning have recently expressed serious doubts whether the judges have the capacity to keep the law up to date. The great American judge Benjamin Cardozo put this difficulty nearly fifty years ago when he spoke of situations where again and again the processes of judge-made law bring judges to a stand they would be glad to abandon if an outlet could be gained.[1] When the doctrine of precedent forces the judges into an impasse nothing but legislation will serve to uproot the ugly or antiquated or unjust rule. But the legislature is usually preoccupied with other things and is informed only intermittently of the needs and problems of the courts. Cardozo saw the legislature and the courts moving on in proud and silent isolation; he urged that some agency must be found to mediate between them, and his call led to the setting up of the New York Law Revision Commission which thirty years later formed the model for our own Law Commissions. Mr Norman Marsh, one of the five English Law Commissioners, discusses this problem and whether the new relationship between the courts, Parliament and the Law Commissions now provides the right balance.

MARSH When I began to study law in the early thirties, it was well established that you could not sue for compensation for

[1]B. Cardozo, *The Nature of the Judicial Process*.

injury if you yourself had been even partially to blame. This meant that where a man had suffered damage partly through his own and partly through another's negligence he was deprived of any remedy at all. The rule, which lawyers call the doctrine of contributory negligence, was generally recognised to be unjust. In continental countries they had a much fairer rule that the courts could reduce the injured person's award to the extent that he himself had contributed to the damage. When the Law Revision Committee reported[1] on the English rule in 1939 they were unable to find any substantial justification for it, but, although the rule was so much criticised, it was not until 1945 that Parliament intervened,[2] in essence by adopting the continental rule.[3] In most of the United States the original rule of the English common law that the contributory negligence of the plaintiff precluded his recovery still prevails to a greater or lesser extent.[4]

This example of a not uncommon situation, when the legal system fails for a long time to respond to the obvious demands of common sense and justice, prompts the question: Is our law too rigid? Every developed system of law must have a static and a dynamic element. The law must be reasonably stable, because one of its principal functions is to provide standards by which people can plan their future conduct. But the law must also be capable of adjustment to new situations and new concepts of human needs. One of the hallmarks of a smoothly

[1]1939 Cmnd. 6032.

[2]See Law Reform (Contributory Negligence) Act 1945.

[3]It is interesting to note that even the continental systems had taken a long time to arrive at this common-sense solution; it first appeared in the Austrian Civil Code of 1811, was applied by the French courts from about the middle of the century, was introduced into Swiss law in 1868, and was not accepted in Germany until the German Civil Code of 1900. See Lawson, *Negligence in the Civil Law*, 19, p. 56.

[4]The effect of contributory negligence is mitigated by the recognition in nearly all jurisdictions in the United States of the doctrine of the 'last clear chance' (see p. 28, n. 1) and by the wide use of juries in civil cases. Also a jury can find that the plaintiff was not guilty of contributory negligence and yet *sub rosa* recognise the existence of contributory negligence by reducing the damages awarded. See Prosser, *Law of Torts*, 2nd ed., p. 296.

working legal system is its built-in capacity to maintain a satisfactory balance between these claims of certainty and of flexibility.

The history of the doctrine of contributory negligence in our law also raises a series of further questions: If the law is too rigid, where does the blame chiefly lie? Is it because the judges are reluctant to develop the principles of the common law and too much inclined to stick to the letter, rather than to seek out the spirit of the statutes? Or is there something wrong with the legislative process of law reform? Our experience with contributory negligence suggests that it is much too simple an answer to put the whole of the blame on the judges. Long before 1945, the courts had shown they were aware of the injustice of the common law rule and had tried to mitigate its effect. But the result was a terrible muddle which confused not only law students but also juries and even judges.[1] A spurious flexibility was purchased at the price of certainty. The truth was that only a clean break with the old rule could remove the injustice, and this only Parliament could achieve.

It may however be suggested that even if English judges have the will to develop and reform the law, they have, owing to the doctrine of binding precedent, been under a special disability which does not exist or is at least less inhibiting in many other systems. Every English lawyer is familiar with cases in which judges have expressed their reluctance in reaching decisions to which they feel compelled by the precedents. It is therefore necessary, in considering what the judges themselves can do to overcome the rigidity of the law and to adapt it to new situations, to take into account the announcement by the Law Lords in 1966 that they would no longer necessarily be bound by one of their earlier decisions.[2] Moreover, the significance of that statement may be greater than appears from its

[1]From 1842 onwards the courts distinguished between contributory negligence, which precluded the plaintiff from recovering damages, and negligence which although in a sense a cause of the accident could be disregarded because the negligent defendant had the 'last clear chance' of avoiding it.

[2][1966] 1 W.L.R.1234.

cautious terms,[1] as the new freedom which the House of Lords has now claimed for itself appears to be having some influence on the attitude of the Court of Appeal to its own earlier decisions.[2] I certainly would not wish to underestimate the potentialities of judicial law-making and law-reforming which are opened up by the Law Lords' statement, especially as already since the statement the House of Lords has declined to follow one of its own leading decisions in an important branch of the law.[3] Nevertheless, I do not think we ought to rely on a coming era of judge-made reforms, not because they are unlikely to materialise but because judge-made law, if it is to be relied upon as the main method of law reform, is inherently unsatisfactory.

In the first place, the reforming decision is quite fortuitous in its operation. The public may have to wait many years before an appropriate opportunity arises in the courts to right an injustice or clarify an obscurity. As Lord Devlin has said, the law has to 'await a litigant with a long purse or the Legal Aid Fund behind him'.[4] Secondly, judge-made reforms, until finally approved at the highest levels, are of uncertain stability. For some years deserted wives thought that they could rely on a certain right or 'equity' in the matrimonial home, a concept which had been developed in a series of cases in the lower courts.

[1]In particular the concluding words: 'This announcement is not intended to affect the use of precedent elsewhere than in this House.'

[2]See *W. & J. B. Eastwood Ltd v. Herrod* [1968] 2 Q.B. 923, especially Lord Denning M.R. at p. 934. See also Lord Denning M.R. in *Gallie v. Lee* [1969] 2 W.L.R. 901 at p. 913; *contra* Russell L.J. at p. 918 and Salmon L.J. at p. 919.

[3]In *Conway v. Rimmer* [1968] A. C. 910 the House of Lords held that where Crown privilege is claimed for a document on the ground that it belongs to a class of documents which it would be contrary to the public interest to produce, the Minister's claim is not necessarily conclusive. If the necessity for secrecy is not obvious, the court may look at the document to decide whether an order shall be made for its production. The remarks of Lord Simon in *Duncan v. Cammell Laird & Co.* [1942] A.C.624, which had been generally taken to mean that the Minister's claim of Crown privilege could not in the last resort be questioned by the court, were disapproved.

[4]*Samples of Lawmaking*, p. 4.

But this security was rudely shaken by a decision of the House of Lords in 1965[1] which exploded the concept. The deserted wife was left unprotected until rescued by an Act of Parliament[2] in 1967. There is a third and to my mind conclusive objection to relying principally on the courts to effect legal reforms. However enlightened the judge, however much he is inspired with reforming zeal, he can only carry out a patching job, restricted as he is by the circumstances of the case before him. If he ventures on principles going much beyond the case before him, he only leaves a heritage of uncertainty for future litigants. Yet perhaps the most important lesson which I have learned in the Law Commission, considering various proposals for reform, is that the fabric of the law is composed of a seamless web. The most minor changes often turn out to have much wider implications than was at first realised. The change may be very necessary, but to effect it much else has to be changed. A judge is seldom in a position, within the limits of the case before him, to take account of all the implications of a new development of the law.[3]

[1]*National Provincial Bank Ltd. v. Ainsworth* [1965] A.C.1175.

[2]Matrimonial Homes Act.

[3]This disadvantage of the judicial position was recognised by the House of Lords in *Suisse Atlantique Société d'Armement Maritime S.A. v. N.V. Rotterdamsche Kolen Centrale* [1967] 1 A.C. 361, where it refused to confirm the existence of a rule of law, independent of the contractual wills of the parties, whereby one party could treat a contract at an end if the other party had committed a 'fundamental breach' of the contract. The doctrine of 'fundamental breach' had been developed in comparatively recent years by the lower courts to provide a remedy for a party who might otherwise find himself bound to carry out his side of an agreement although the other party by a skilfully worded 'exemption clause' was provided with an excuse for the non-performance of some essential part of his side of the agreement. As Lord Reid (at p. 406) pointed out, to speak in terms of 'fundamental breach' did not get to the heart of the problem, which lay in the equality or non-equality of the parties as regards their bargaining position when making an agreement containing an 'exemption clause'. 'This is a complex problem,' he concluded, 'which affects millions of people and it appears to me that the solution should be left to Parliament.' The Law Commissioners have now made proposals (Law Com. 24; Scot. Law Com. 12) with regard to clauses exempting from liability under ss. 12-15 of the Sale of Goods Act 1893.

Finally, it must be remembered that a judicial decision which involves a desirable development of the law may be very unjust to one of the parties before the court. He may arrange his affairs in reliance on the law as it was thought to be, and then suddenly find that the courts have in effect changed the law retrospectively. It was doubtless this which led the Law Lords to add to their announcement in 1966 the statement that they would 'bear in mind the danger of disturbing retrospectively the basis on which contracts, settlements of property and fiscal arrangements have been entered into and also the especial need for certainty as to the criminal law'.

If this catalogue of the deficiencies of judicial law-making as a method of law reform suggests that it ought to be carried out by legislation, I also recognise that law reform by legislation has its own problems. The chief problem has been the difficulty of getting it through Parliament. Governments, irrespective of party, have on the whole been reluctant to allow parliamentary time for law reform. This is not necessarily because it is regarded as undesirable in itself. It is partly because law reform seldom wins a government much political credit; it also takes up valuable time which is needed for more politically controversial items in the Government's programme. And the Opposition may not be slow to spin out that time even on an inherently non-controversial measure, if it is likely to create difficulties for other legislation which the Government really wants and to which the Opposition with equal conviction is opposed. When that kind of situation arises, a small but determined interest-group which fears disadvantage to its members in a particular law reform measure may wield a delaying power out of all proportion to its real importance.

Another problem is that, even when time is found for law reform legislation, there is seldom enough time to allow a deep-searching investigation of all the technical, social and economic implications. Before the Law Commissions were set up in 1965, such an investigation was sometimes carried out, before the introduction of the legislation, by a departmental or specialist law reform committee or Royal Commission. But as the members of such bodies sat on a part-time and voluntary basis, and usually had limited research facilities, the scope and speed of their work was inevitably restricted. A third problem arises from the piecemeal character of the law reform measures that are in fact passed; reforms, good in themselves, may tend to complicate rather than to simplify the law as a whole. I should add that this has a side effect on law-making by the judges. Many statutes, even those with a reforming aim, give the judges no clear indications of principle, from which the law can be expanded and adjusted to deal with new situations.

However, I think the present outlook is more hopeful, not only for law reform by legislation but also, within its inherent limits, for judicial law-making. The Law Commissions now have a general responsibility for the 'systematic development and reform'[1] of the law. Their own reports, and those of the bodies to whom particular topics have been referred on the Commissions' recommendation, can, or at least should, be prepared as a part of a wider plan for the law as a whole. This does not mean that the Law Commissions cannot, and indeed do not deal with minor adjustments of the law – with what might be called its 'running repairs'; in the past these have been too easily overlooked and neglected. But as the Commissions' Reports come before Parliament they should ease the passing of the implementing legislation in two ways: first, Parliament will know that the proposed changes have been examined and explained by an independent and non-political body, after wide consultation with the interests affected; secondly, Parliament will have some assurance that the particular proposals form part of a wider plan for the coherent development of the law.

Yet it would be quite unrealistic to suggest that the existence of the Law Commissions will alone overcome the difficulties of getting reform legislation through Parliament. To the extent that their proposals are recognised as desirable and, from a party political point of view, uncontroversial, it may be possible to facilitate their passing into law by a somewhat simplified parliamentary procedure. A beginning has been made with the

[1]Law Commissions Act 1965, s. 3.

device of a Second Reading Committee in the House of Commons, which makes it possible to debate a Bill at that stage in Committee rather than on the floor of the House. But in the long run, when major law reform measures[1] come before Parliament, especially those which inevitably raise difficult issues of social policy, I think more fundamental changes in the parliamentary process of law-making will have to be considered. What we notably lack, in contrast to many other countries, is an expert committee of parliamentarians, which, on the introduction of a Bill, can examine it in depth, perhaps hearing evidence from outside Parliament, and which can ultimately present it to the whole House with a reasoned explanation and justification of its provisions.

Parliament and the judges should not however be considered as mutually exclusive sources of law reform. If I suggest that the main impetus should come from Parliament, I also recognise that the judges, in interpreting the statutes, will continue to play a vital part in maintaining a satisfactory balance between the flexibility and certainty of the law. But more could be done to assist the judges in this task. They could be freed from some of the self-imposed restrictions which, for instance, sometimes prevent them from looking at a Royal Commission report when interpreting a statute based on that report. They could also be provided with material to assist them in interpreting the statutes.[2]

As more of our law is embodied in comprehensive codes, it will obviously be impossible to legislate specifically for every case which may arise. Yet to leave the courts room to apply the law to new situations does not necessarily mean that the law will be uncertain, if the principles on which it is intended to develop are reasonably clear. A commentary on a code, for example, to which the courts might refer when faced with difficult problems of interpretation could throw light on these basic principles of growth; it would not necessarily be embodied

[1]As, for example, the Contract, Landlord & Tenant and Criminal Law Codes on which the Law Commission is now engaged.

[2]A Joint Report of the English and Scottish Law Commissions on the Interpretation of Statutes making such proposals (Law Com. 21; Scot. Law Com. 11) was published in June 1969.

in the code itself, because what the citizen and his legal adviser primarily want in a code is an uncluttered and clear statement of the law covering the ordinary case. But such a commentary could be a valuable guide when problems arise which were not, and perhaps could not have been, anticipated by the draftsman.

Moreover, there may be ways of mitigating, if not of eliminating, the inherent defects of case law as a method of developing the law. It might be possible to reduce the fortuitous character of this method of law reform if we were prepared to provide State funds to pay the costs of litigants – and not merely of poor litigants – in cases where a decision of the House of Lords on a point of public interest would help to clarify the law; a scheme of this type is already in force in some Australian States.[1] And we can accelerate and cheapen such decisions of the House of Lords by providing machinery for sending appropriate cases direct from the trial court to the House of Lords, 'leap-frogging' the intermediate appeal courts. This proposal was in fact made by the Evershed Committee in 1953 and has now been adopted in Part II of the Administration of Justice Act in 1969. There is also the possibility of reducing the element of unfairness which a desirable development of the law by the courts may bring to a litigant who has quite reasonably relied on earlier decisions: one way would be for a court to make a rule for future cases, while judging the rights of the parties

[1]Some particulars of the scheme in force in New South Wales under the Suitor's Fund Act 1951 (as amended by Acts of 1959 and 1960) and in Victoria under the Appeal Costs Fund Act of 1964 are given in the paper by Marshall and Marsh, 'Case Law, Codification and Statute Law Revision' in *Record of the Third Commonwealth and Empire Law Conference*, 1965 (London: Sweet & Maxwell, 1966), p. 407 and pp. 432–3. The New South Wales scheme in its initial form was commented on by the Evershed Committee (see *Report of the Committee on Supreme Court Practice and Procedure*, 1953 Cmnd 8878, paragraphs 634–5). They suggested that the scheme, although outside their terms of reference, might be later considered with a view to its suitability for the United Kingdom, but the suggestion has not yet been taken up. A broader version of the same proposal was made by the Law Society in a memorandum in 1964 (*Law Society's Annual Report* 1963–4, pp. 77–80). See also *Proposals for Suitors Fund* by *Justice*, April 1969.

before the court on the basis of the previously existing law. This device of prospective over-ruling is well established in the Supreme Court of the United States and has recently been copied by the Indian Supreme Court.[1]

The doctors of an earlier age sought to find an elixir of life which would reconcile the conflicting humours or temperaments of the human body. We are not likely to be any more successful in our legal system. But I think we can have rather more certainty and a greater measure of flexibility if we improve, and develop the improvements that have already been made in, the techniques of law reform by legislation, and if we make better provision for the judicial development by the courts of the resulting legislation.

[1]See an informative review of the relevant American cases and of the implications of the leading case in which the Indian Supreme Court followed the American device (*Golak Nath v. State of Punjab* [1967] 2 S.C.R.762; A.I.R.1967 S.C.1643) by W. S. Hooker Jr. in (*1967*) *9 Journal of the Indian Law Institute* 596.

DOES THE LAW ADEQUATELY PROTECT THE INDIVIDUAL AGAINST THE STATE?

J. R. WARREN EVANS

ZANDER Compared with other countries of European cultural descent, we have made relatively little use of law as a means of protecting the individual against the state. We have no protection against wrongs done by Parliament. We have no code of individual rights which even the legislature must respect and our courts have no power to question the constitutionality of any Act of Parliament. We have very limited protection against wrongs done by civil servants and other administrative bodies. There are few grounds on which the individual is entitled to challenge administrative decisions in the courts and, even where there is a ground of challenge, the courts have only limited powers to give a remedy. During the past few years there has begun to be increasing interest in this problem. The establishment of the Ombudsman was a concrete expression of this growing concern. But the more usual English approach to these questions is that the control of legislation should be left exclusively to parliament, that the work of the public administration should not be held up by legal proceedings and that the administrators should be left to put their own wrongs right – prodded here and there by Members of Parliament but without being subject to the interference of the lawyers. The question that Mr Warren Evans, a barrister, discusses is whether this traditional view needs modification and whether the law adequately protects the individual against the state.

WARREN EVANS The most important thing about this question is that it is being asked in this form. For even before an attempt is made to answer it, it directs attention to two important assumptions – first, that the individual is in fact in need of protection, not only against other individuals and private organisations, but also against the public institutions of the society in which he lives, and secondly, that the law provides a means by which he may, perhaps even should, be protected. These are political assumptions, in the broadest sense of political, and they are very widely shared in this country – but they are none the less important for that, and before I give my answer to this question, I want to say a word about them.

First then, the need for protection. What is it precisely that the individual needs protecting against? It is obviously too vague to talk about protection against 'the state' in general: what we mean is the protection of the individual against the kind of wrongs which can be done to him by the many different organisations which are referred to collectively as 'the state'. The question is also directed to those wrongs which it is peculiarly within the power of the state to inflict: the individual may be wronged by being carelessly run over by a post office van, but that is not what we mean by this question. On the other hand, where there is a public telephone monopoly, the arbitrary and wrongful withdrawal of telephone services is certainly a wrong peculiarly within the power of the state to inflict. The wrongs of which the state is capable vary greatly from institution to institution whether one is talking, for example, about the legislature, the judiciary, or the executive. In each case one must be careful to identify and describe the wrong – for only then can one go on to ask what provision is made or ought to be made to protect the individual against it. One further word about protection: the word is used, and I shall use it here, to describe both steps taken to ensure that a wrong is not done at all, and steps taken to put a wrong right once it has been done, by the payment of compensation or other means.

The second important assumption is that the law provides an effective and desirable way of giving the individual protection against these wrongs. By 'the law' in this context I understand the system of rules and rights which are enforceable, directly or indirectly, in the courts. Now some would say: 'But that's self-evident: that is what the law is surely about'. It is by no means so obvious. As Michael Zander has already pointed out, England has in fact made very little use of law as a means of protecting the individual against the state. I would merely emphasise that even where there is an undoubted need to protect the individual against wrongs done by public institutions, it remains an open question, a matter of choice, as to which method or methods of protection should be employed.

I must now face up to the question restated in conventional constitutional terms: Does the law adequately protect the individual against the legislature – that is Parliament, against the authorities administering justice, and against the executive, or, as I prefer to call them, administrative authorities generally?

My answer to the first, about the legislature, is: No – but. There is no specific protection under the law against wrongs done by the legislature: the individual's security lies in the efficient operation of a democratic legislative process. The absence of legal protection in this field is not however popularly regarded as a defect of our system, though there is a growing body of informed opinion in favour of the introduction of a Bill of Rights, embodying certain key individual rights, to which even ordinary legislation would have to conform. I do not therefore propose to deal with this question at length.

My answer to the second question, whether the law adequately protects the individual against those responsible for the administration of justice, is: Yes – but. English law and English lawyers have been highly successful in developing safeguards against the abuse of power by the judiciary and by the police – though less successful, I think, in regulating the exercise of power by prison authorities. There is in this country, both within the legal profession and outside, a highly developed sensitivity to certain types of wrong of which institutions in this field are capable: for example, wrongful arrest and imprisonment, wrongful or unfair police interrogation, the wrongful exercise of powers of search, and unfairness in the conduct of trials, particularly criminal trials.

Nevertheless, in spite of that success, there are certain

wrongs against which I think the individual is still inadequately protected. I would name three.

First, the wrong of the unjust sentence. Far too little time is spent by lawyers and judges in court in dealing with matters of sentencing, and in ensuring consistency between sentences. Much has been done in recent years to reduce the chances of injustice in sentencing. But I believe further checks should be built into the system: it should be a rule of law, for instance, that sentence should not be pronounced on the same day as the trial, so as to give proper time for reflection. There should be an end to the odd convention that advocates should not mention the actual length of the possible sentence when addressing the judge. I should like to see discussion in open court about the sentence, including comparisons with other sentences. There ought to be fuller discussion too between the lawyers and the psychiatrists, where appropriate. And in order to minimise the effects of a wrong decision once it has been taken, it ought to be made easier to obtain bail pending the hearing of an appeal.

Then there is the wrong of having to go through legal proceedings without legal representation, particularly in criminal proceedings, and particularly where there is the possibility of imprisonment. Here again there has been much progress in the last twenty years: this wrong has virtually been eliminated from jury trials in criminal cases, both at Quarter Sessions and at Assizes. But there remain the magistrates' courts, which are of increasing importance in the administration of justice, and before which the individual too frequently has to go without a lawyer, either because of his own ignorance or timidity, or because of the restrictive policies of particular courts in granting legal aid.

Thirdly, there are the wrongs done by prosecuting authorities in the exercise of their powers. This is something to which we in this country are very insensitive: by this country, I mean England and Wales, for Scotland has quite a different system. I do not suggest that wrongs are frequently done by those conducting prosecutions: but a wrong is sometimes done when a prosecution is launched on insufficient evidence; and a wrong is also done where a prosecutor lets an accused off too lightly, as for example where he allows a serious charge to be dealt with by magistrates when it should, in the interests of those harmed by the crime, be dealt with by a superior court with greater sentencing powers. The great weakness of the English system is that most prosecutions are brought and conducted by the police themselves. I believe that the individual would be better protected if the prosecuting function were taken away from the police altogether and given to the Director of Public Prosecutions; the police would also be freed for tasks of investigation and detection, to which their organisation is better suited and for which they are already undermanned.

I come now to the last question: Does the law adequately protect the individual against wrongs done by administrative authorities? And here my answer is unequivocal: No, it does not. But let me first satisfy my own test and identify the wrongs I am talking about. I mean the situation in which the individual is harmed by conduct on the part of public authorities which is incompetent or careless, ill-informed, unfair, or simply not in accordance with the law as laid down by Parliament. The protection which the law does offer in this field takes many different forms, and in order to make any overall judgement it is essential to take them all into account. For example, certain administrative functions are actually exercised by tribunals or committees which are themselves independent of the ordinary administrative authorities. They hold public hearings before they reach a decision; this is common for instance in the licensing field, for pubs, betting shops, dance halls. The law may also provide in other circumstances for the individual to be given a hearing before the decision is made, a hearing either by the administrative authority that is going to make the decision, or by an independent tribunal with power to make recommendations to that authority. And then after the decision is made, the law sometimes gives an 'open-ended' right of appeal, either to a court, or to a special independent tribunal like a national insurance or industrial tribunal, or to a superior administrative authority – such as where an appeal lies from a local authority to the Ministry of Housing and Local Government in planning matters. By 'open-ended' I mean that the appeal body, whether it is a tribunal or a superior administrative authority or even a court, has the power to take the administrative decision all over again, substituting its own view for that of the first authority. And even when such special rights of appeal have been exhausted, there remain two further possibilities: first, there is the possibility of an enquiry by the Ombudsman (the Parliamentary Commissioner for Administration), and secondly, there is an appeal to a court on the ground that the administrative decision is bad in law. This last form of protection, which is in one sense fundamental to the operation of any system of protection under law, is not well developed in this country. The tendency has been for Parliament to rely on providing one or more of the other forms of protection I have described, and to cut down the opportunities for challenge in the courts.

But how is it, one may ask, that with such a range of opportunities, it can possibly be said that the individual's overall protection is inadequate? The inadequacy lies beneath the surface, in the actual use that has been made by Parliament of these protective techniques in legislation, and in the limits that there are in practice upon their use by individuals. For instance, the value of administrative tribunals is severely limited by the fact that there is no legal aid available for tribunal proceedings. Although the government has had power to provide legal aid since 1949, it has never done so; and the value of pre-decision hearings can be easily undermined by the absence of any recognised rules of procedure. In any case, when you have such a hearing the authority is not usually bound by the views of those who conduct the hearing. Again, the value of the Ombudsman is limited by the exclusion of the individual from the actual process of inquiry – there is no right to a hearing nor any right to a remedy – and also by the fact that the Ombudsman has no power at all to investigate maladministration at the local government level. And the value of a right of appeal to the courts is in practice often very limited, limited for instance by the difficulty of obtaining an adequate statement of reasons from the administrative authority, or by the presence in the legislation itself of very vaguely defined powers, or by the difficulties of obtaining damages for administrative wrongs, or simply and frequently by the costs and likely delay involved in court proceedings.

Lastly, and very important indeed, there are a substantial number of administrative decisions to which none of the special forms of protection apply at all, and in which rights of appeal to the courts are very restricted indeed. This is true of the administration of immigration control, for example, and of decisions taken by the Board of Trade in the field of economic regulation, of local authority distributive decisions in such matters as the allocation of council housing, and of certain administrative decisions in the field of education and in the National Health Service.

Now, can anything be done about this? I think it can. Parliament should enact a general code of administrative procedure binding on all administrative authorities, central and local, and the courts should be given power to enforce that code. It is quite true that a wrong decision may be taken even where an authority is correctly informed and the individual has fully explained his case. But the chances of a wrong being done are far less where a fair procedure has been adopted. Indeed it is in the public as well as in the individual's interest that the public administration should be conducted fairly and openly, and in accordance with certain well-tested principles of good administration. Our very concept of legality should be expanded to include adherence to those principles, so that a decision reached other than in accordance with them would be regarded as invalid or illegal. This does not mean that an offending decision would necessarily have to be cancelled or, in legal terms, annulled: the courts could be given the power to allow the decision to stand, so that the work of the administration should not be unduly disrupted, and also the power to compensate the individual financially if that course were taken. It should also be made clear by legislation that damages can be awarded for the insecurity, worry and inconvenience that can be caused to the individual by maladministration, even where he sustains no demonstrable loss in terms of money or other property.

There would, I believe, be general agreement on the principles to be included in such a code. There should be a general time-limit upon administrative decisions; authorities should be under a duty to state the reasons for their decisions. They would also be under a duty to make all necessary factual inquiries before the decision was made; they would be required to provide maximum opportunities for pre-decision hearings and representations, and to give proper publicity to their own decisions. The legislation could also develop other rules of English administrative law which are seriously defective: for instance, it should give the courts power to annul an administrative decision taken on the basis of facts which are not materially correct.

The object would be to ensure high standards of fair administration, and to allow the individual to use the courts to ensure that those standards were observed in his case. It might well be necessary to reorganise the courts in certain respects to enable them to perform this function. And a code of administrative procedure would not be the whole answer; I do not propose it as such: there would still be a need to improve the other forms of protection, and the need for vigilance in the creation of new executive powers. But with these changes, there is no doubt that the individual would be far better protected against the state than he is at present.

THE LEGAL PROFESSION

MORRIS FINER, Q.C.

ZANDER A series about the defects of the law ought also to look at the lawyers who administer it. It is true that practising lawyers do not make the law and in one sense it may therefore be unfair to blame them for its shortcomings. But the lawyers are the high priests who guard the mysteries of the art and at least in so far as they fail to exert themselves to see that the faults are corrected they can properly be made to shoulder some part of the responsibility. Also, in some of their rules and attitudes they embody the very defects of which the layman complains – especially perhaps in their restrictive practices which have so often been in the news in the last few years. The profession is today being required to explain and justify itself not only to a critical Press and the public at large but for the first time more specifically to independent bodies such as the Prices and Incomes Board, which has investigated solicitors' fees, and the Monopolies Commission, which is at present examining restrictive practices in all the professions. It is striking that both sides of the profession have responded to this pressure by appointing public relations firms to help improve their image. Even ten years ago this would have been unthinkable. But in spite of some stirrings of reform from within, the profession remains extremely reluctant to change. Both barristers and solicitors in their official evidence to the Monopolies Commission, for instance, presented arguments justifying the *status quo* without conceding at any point that there was any need for reform or even that the critics of the profession have a case that at least requires an answer. Mr Morris Finer, Q.C., considers whether the profession can both meet the demand that it brings itself up to date and at the same time preserve its standards.

FINER Lawyers have never won a prize in the popularity stakes. It is a safe prediction that they never will. One has merely to speak of the *profession* of law, to detect that one has offended against the instinct that justice ought not to stand in need of the services of a middleman. The lawyer is an intruder into Eden; his presence an affront to the vision which men carry within them of a paradise lost, and hopefully to be regained, in which lambs and lions will congregate without specialist assistance. The philosophical practitioner of the law accepts the point. He acknowledges his role as victim of the yearning for a Golden Age, as a fomentor of that tension which is bound to arise between the individual's feeling for justice and society's need for law.

But there is a different, much more specific and relevant sense in which the legal profession comes under suspicion in Britain today. It has to do with a process which, I suspect, is much the same as that which has led to a critical public attitude towards the professions in general. People are doubting whether the idea of a profession, as something established in and received from the past, is adequate to meet the requirements of a modern society.

Originally, in Greece and early Rome, the lawyer was a patrician whose pursuit of the law was one of the means by which he promoted his own search for the life of virtue. The advocate was engaged in an enterprise whose reward was the moral satisfaction and merit he won for himself, rather than the victories he won for his client. The professionalisation of the lawyer, and of his relationship with his client, was the slow growth of later ages. In England, it involved the establishment of a division of the legal profession into two branches – the barristers and the solicitors. The process reached its culmination in Victorian times. Each branch of the profession evolved its own tight organisation. Each organisation laid down its own strict standards for entry. Both established detailed codes of regulations and practice to govern their dealings with the public and with each other.

The essence of this evolution was the working out and

imposition of restrictive practices: entry by examination; a defined sphere of monopolistic operation for those who have passed through the barrier; rules as to what is permissible, and what is not, in the relationship between barrister and solicitor, and between each of them and his clients. And at a time when 'restrictive practice' has become all but unmentionable, it is important to stress that, in the professional context, it was precisely as a result of these practices that standards were established which are still, by common consent, second in quality to none in the world.

Of course, restrictive practices benefited the profession. But also they were the framework within which lawyers became free to institutionalise a set of ethical imperatives. Behind these defences, those things which society rightly felt to be moral necessities – a fair guarantee of competence on the part of the lawyer, the certainty of his honesty and independence, his reliability in all matters arising from the relationship of trust between himself and his client – could be translated by the lawyers into working and binding rules. As R. H. Tawney has put it:

> It is significant that at a time when the professional classes had defined free competition as the arbiter of commerce and industry, they did not dream of applying it to the occupations in which they were themselves primarily interested, but maintained, and, indeed, elaborated machinery through which a professional conscience might find expression.

But there was another aspect of this development. Essentially all of it took place in the matrix of an individualistic society in which the lawyer's clients were the landowner, the farmer, the trustee of the marriage settlement, the employer and the company promoter. It was a society in which two categories of right – property and freedom of contract – were paramount. The lawyer served to protect these rights, and his profession took its tone and outlook from the wealthy and middle classes who were principally concerned with them.

Times have very much changed. We live in a welfare society. Public opinion has demanded and Parliament has provided that property and freedom of contract shall not always dominate all other rights. We have enacted new rights in protection of the poor and the sick, the young and the old, the weak and disadvantaged of all sorts. We have given legal sanction to the notion of public interest as against private interest in many fields. We have established as agencies, through which to apply and enforce much of this new and ever-increasing law, a vast apparatus of tribunals and procedures which bear little resemblance to the courts and procedures to which lawyers are accustomed and in which they have developed their traditional skills.

I suggest that we have now arrived at the crux of the problem which confronts the contemporary practising lawyer. Can a profession whose ideology and organisation crystallised during an era of outstandingly successful service to the needs of an individualistic society adapt itself, with like success, to the needs of the welfare state? Can it do so without damaging its hard-won values of independence for itself and exclusive commitment to the interests of its clients? Will it find the courage and the energy to do so from its own resources, or must it suffer impatient surgery at the hands of those who know more about the pain than the cure?

I believe that it is questions such as these, and an unease as to the ability or willingness of the lawyers to tackle them, which offer the real contemporary challenge to the profession. I think that the challenge can be met. It would be too much to say that a wind of change is roaring down the ancient corridors. But there is a distinct current of fresh air. Certainly, the governing bodies and some respected practitioners on both sides of the profession are showing themselves to be sensitive to the need for adaptation to a changed society. This may partly be no more than a shrewd defensive response. But it does also reflect the growth of an intelligent realisation and real conviction that we cannot produce a twentieth-century service from an unaltered nineteenth-century mould. This realisation has not spread as far down to the grass roots of the profession as it is essential for it to go. The lawyer, almost irrespective of his politics, is by training and self-interest a conservative in the affairs of his own profession. The *status quo* is part of his mental capital. Every legal reform robs him of an asset he has worked hard to acquire. Nevertheless, no one who has swum in the climate of professional opinion over the last five years can fail to be aware of a growth, during that time, of a reforming spirit greater than any which emerged over the whole of several preceding decades.

What then has to be done? Even at the simple level of office organisation and business efficiency the answer is: a good deal. I hardly exaggerate if I recall one prominent colleague who, in midwinter, amid an indescribable confusion of Victorian furniture and a popping noise from the one remaining element in an antediluvian gas fire, took pleasure in expounding the law to a throng of City bankers turned literally blue with cold, while he himself sat clad in mittens and an overcoat. I do not present this as an endearing Dickensian eccentricity. Lawyers and their staffs form a significant part of the national economy, and it is unfair to the consumer, and a reproach to the lawyer, if he cannot manage his concern any more efficiently than a third-rate pickle factory.

Consumer-orientation may be a provocative phrase to use to a profession which devotes its working life, and much of what for others would be leisure time, to devising the best means to produce the maximum satisfaction of its clientele. But we need much more of it. The lawyer's consciousness of his inner rectitude – a phenomenon which afflicts the Bar more peculiarly than it does the solicitors' branch – is no substitute. It is apt, indeed, to communicate itself to the lay public as an aloofness, or worse still, a pomposity, which they find it hard to bear. A more educated population is less inclined than its ancestors – and rightly so – to prostrate itself before the witch doctor, however remarkable his spells.

These matters relate to the 'image' of the profession, and they have an importance. I have referred to the constructive role of the restrictive practice. That does not diminish the urgency for scraping the barnacles, so long as we take care of the timbers beneath.

But there are, to my mind, more fundamental matters to which the profession needs to address itself. If the practising lawyer is to cope with the needs of a changing society, he must rescue himself from the self-imposed intellectual limitations which insulate him from appreciating those needs. As things are, he is cut off even from his fellow-lawyers who are not in private practice to an extent which obtains nowhere else in the world. It is common in America for a good lawyer to teach at a university, then to become a partner in a law firm, then to join a government agency, or a big corporation, or to do all these things in some other order. This produces a cross-fertilisation of experience which is almost unknown in this country. We must do much more to open the lines of communication and exchange between the different breeds of our own species. And, while I personally think that the fusion of the two branches of the profession would produce more public ill than good, even so we must find ways of making it much easier to change from being a barrister to a solicitor, or vice versa.

Enlarging the mental horizons of the lawyer presupposes major reforms in our system of legal education. There is now a well-supported movement to rationalise an educational system which is inefficiently divided between the universities, the Bar and the Law Society. The profession must produce lawyers – not statisticians, or sociologists, or welfare workers. Training must guarantee a proper level of technical competence. But the law operates in a particular social setting with a view to meeting needs and adjusting conflicts in a manner conformable with current facts and values. Thus, we cannot afford to train lawyers who are sealed off from the related disciplines; who are very good at reading but very bad at counting; who pick up precedents as though they were rules, not tools; and in whom we nurture the illusion that law is some pleasant and leafy retreat in place of an understanding of law as the teeming, open-ende avenue through which most of the traffic of contemporary existence passes.

The profession has done much, through the legal aid and advice scheme, to help the casualities of that traffic. But if the professional ideal is to demonstrate its capacity to stretch to the modern condition, the most important proof of it will be the ability of lawyers to minimise the number of those casualties who still go short of legal assistance. The lawyers must positively reach out to all those sections of the population whose way of life has not taught them the self-preserving instinct of calling on the family solicitor when they anticipate or encounter trouble. There are thousands of people who, when threatened with eviction, or denied a pension, or accused of shoplifting, or involved in any other of the crisis-laden situations which life is apt to inflict on them, still do not know what to do, or where or to whom to turn. The welfare state has given them rights; it is the responsibility of the legal profession to do all in its power to ensure that the individual shall have the opportunity to exercise those rights. The legal profession must actively search for the means to achieve this purpose, and must be strong in the determination not to be obstructed by ingrained customs derived from the past.

The truth is that there is no incompatibility between what the society in which he lives demands of the contemporary lawyer and what his received professional ideals also demand of him. The welfare state gives more, not less, room for the maintenance and expansion of the professional spirit. As the scope for service broadens, and the number of those with claims to service multiply; as the dominant concept enlarges from palliation of need to the provision of satisfactions; as rights take over from privileges – so does it become increasingly important to guarantee confidence in all the professions. It is true enough that the civil service, and business itself, for example the banks, have taken over many of the functions that used to be performed by lawyers. But the success which these new agencies have achieved is in direct proportion to the extent to which they have themselves managed to achieve professional competence. The legal profession, if it can spur itself on with its own values, need feel at no disadvantage in this regard. There is as much room and necessity as at any time in the past – in fact, in the era of the all-powerful state, much more – for the preservation of those values. A tradition is not all disadvantage. And the courageous lawyer will find that there are no insuperable problems in adapting his own traditions to the needs of the world around him.

SHOULD ACCIDENT CASES BE TAKEN AWAY FROM THE COURTS?

HARRY STREET

ZANDER This question raises the problem of the efficiency of the legal system. Professor Street of the University of Manchester explains why he believes that it might be cheaper and quicker, as well as more just, for compensation for injuries suffered in accidents to be handled away from the courts by other kinds of bodies. The question is important not only because the courts have done this business for centuries but also because personal injuries litigation today accounts for no less than eighty per cent of the business of the Queen's Bench Division of the High Court. The loss of all this work would therefore be a serious blow to the legal profession. But the threat to the profession is obviously only one of the considerations; much more important is whether such a major change would work to the overall public advantage. The problem is also important as an example of other questions that are just beginning to be asked. Solicitors, for instance, derive over half their income from conveyancing; yet the day may not be far distant when a computerised system of registration could make the lawyer's role in the process of land transfer largely redundant. Not that lawyers should ever find themselves without work. On the contrary, the complexity of the modern welfare state is such that there is probably a considerable unmet need for professional legal services among all sections of the public. The first step however towards a rethinking of the role of lawyers in modern society is the kind of analysis of the pros and cons of the present system done by Professor Street in relation to accident claims.

STREET Millions of people are injured every year in accidents in this country. What redress have they? If they can show that the accident was caused by another's negligence the courts will award damages to them against the person responsible. You may say: 'What could be fairer than that?' But let us look at the matter.

It does not mean that all victims are compensated. To succeed they must prove negligence. That is not so easy as it sounds, especially when one remembers that the trial might be years after the accident. Take a motoring collision. Is every witness, even if he is traced, going to remember exactly what happened years ago? Will the defendant motorist and his passengers tell the whole truth? It is difficult enough for a disinterested witness to give a complete account of a collision, even immediately after it happened. Too often the victim will not even be able to produce bystanders in court as witnesses: common observation shows that many witnesses of road accidents – particularly passing motorists – hasten from the scene for the express purpose of 'not getting involved'; whereas the witness of a murder is likely to be a reliable witness – the happening is unique in his experience and the details are firmly etched in his mind – we all see traffic movement throughout our lives, and we neither perceive nor retain details of the commonplace with comparable facility. Suppose the true facts are arrived at. It is still not always simple to say whether there was negligence. Negligence has nothing to do with moral fault; the court has to lay down what a reasonable man should have foreseen and then decide whether the defendant fell below that standard. When is it negligent for a motorist on a major road, when approaching a minor crossing, not to brake sharply enough to avoid colliding with a car which does not halt on reaching the major road as it travels along the minor one? When should the reasonable motorist be able to correct a skid without losing control of his vehicle? When he is dazzled by the headlights of an approaching car, is he negligent unless he at once brakes so sharply that he can avoid hitting anything there may be within the limited range of his now blurred vision?

In practice only a small proportion of accident victims obtain an adequate remedy. Most will be unable to prove negligence.

Many who do prove it fall foul of another law: that compensation is reduced to the extent that the victim is also at fault. Again, a man who is sued can offer to settle the action by paying money into court before trial. As a result, a lot of people who might have won their case settle it before trial for a sum very much smaller than they would have received had the court found in their favour. They do this for, if they eventually lose, or are awarded less damages than the defendant has already paid into court, they have to pay all their own legal fees and the other side's as well. Victims of trivial accidents fare better on settlements because small claims have a nuisance value to insurance companies, who prefer to settle them quickly.

Some victims then are compensated to some extent through the courts by those proved to be at fault, but there is nothing for the rest. We have to ask other questions about the present system. Is it efficient? Does it operate quickly and cheaply? No. The average period between an accident and judgement in a contested High Court case is over two years. Look at the expenses in traffic cases. Motorists have to insure with insurance companies or Lloyd's against the risk of accidents. Statistics show that commission to agents and the other expenses incurred by insurance companies are about fifty per cent of the sums they pay out on claims. Add to that lawyers' fees, judges' salaries and the cost of maintaining courts, and we see that the combined costs of insurance and court proceedings add up to more than the net benefits which reach the victims.

Why give cash to an accident victim? Well, suddenly he is deprived of his wages, yet his bills mount up and his commitments for rent and hire purchase run on. He needs cash straightaway in place of his lost earnings, but he gets nothing till his action is disposed of – that may be years too late. Then all he receives is a lump sum, and there is nothing to stop him from 'blueing it' in a few weeks, leaving it to the state to maintain him.

The courts developed our law of negligence in an age when social security was unknown, when an award of damages was the only means of making good the loss. The court action no longer meets his hospital and medical requirements – he mostly relies on the National Health Service. Payment is too late to meet his pressing financial needs – he has to turn instead to the Ministry of Social Security for prompt payment of sickness benefit. For example, an insured person earning eighteen pounds a week and having a wife and three children gets over twelve pounds a week in benefit at once. The present common-law system is endurable only because it is propped up at every stage by the welfare state.

Another object should be to rehabilitate victims. The court action does nothing about this; indeed it discourages it. The claimant who appears in court with a useless cut-off ugly stump of an arm may fare better than one who has gone to the trouble of obtaining an artificial limb. In theory the court could award the cost of private treatment for rehabilitation, but this rarely happens. Medical rehabilitation is left to the National Health Service, and the Department of Employment and Productivity sees to vocational rehabilitation. So, to sum up the present arrangements, it is a matter of chance whether victims obtain any damages; the more serious the accident the greater the likelihood that the compensation will be inadequate; the cash does not arrive when it is most needed; the expenses are enormous; it is wasteful and slow and does nothing to promote standards of safety.

In 1966 the government appointed a high-powered committee of judges and practising lawyers to recommend how these court procedures could be improved. After years of deliberation their proposals[1] are so meagre and so marginal that in a negative way they mark the futility of merely tinkering with the present common-law system. If these changes are the best that can be managed under the present system, we should look elsewhere for our answers.

It is not surprising, then, that other ways of handling accident cases have been devised. Best known are the arrangements we have had since 1946 for dealing with accidents at work. Until

[1]Report of the Committee on Personal Injuries (Winn Committee) Cmnd. 3691, 1968.

then workmen could only take their employers, or rather their employers' insurance companies, to court for workmen's compensation. That old workmen's compensation scheme was a failure; the courts took too long to decide cases, they made the law very complicated, and lawyers had a field day as countless cases were fought on appeal, often all the way to the House of Lords, by the insurance companies. Injured workmen ran the risk of eventually losing their cases and being saddled with heavy legal costs as well. The Beveridge Report in 1942 therefore recommended the scrapping of this system. The war-time Coalition Government agreed, and the necessary legislation was finally enacted in 1946.

A citizen is now entitled to industrial injury benefit whenever he suffers personal injury by an accident arising out of and in the course of his employment. A medical board decides whether the accident caused physical harm and assesses the degree of disablement. Armed with the medical report, officials of the Ministry of Social Security, known as insurance officers, then decide all claims for benefit. A disappointed claimant may appeal to a local tribunal, which consists of a legally qualified chairman and two laymen. There is a further appeal to a National Insurance Commissioner, a full-time official who is a barrister. This scheme has worked very well. Claims are met regardless of whether the employer has been negligent. Cases are decided promptly, perhaps six to ten times as quickly as court accident cases. The contrast between the cost of ordinary court actions and these is astonishing – the expenses, including all the costs of determining disputed claims, are less than ten per cent of the benefits paid to victims. Benefit is paid straightaway in weekly payments so long as the disability lasts. Here we have a system for compensating accident victims which has now operated satisfactorily for over twenty years. It is cheap and quick, it enjoys public confidence, and pays out benefits so as to meet needs as they arise.

Five years ago the inadequacies of the common law compelled us to introduce a fresh scheme for compensating another group of injured citizens: those who are victims of crimes of violence.

All the common law did was to say that if the victim could identify his assailant he could sue him for assault and battery – and little chance he would have of collecting damages from him, even if he managed to identify him. Here again, the new scheme was not entrusted to the courts, and the common-law rules were discarded. The state is now liable to pay compensation to those who suffer personal injury attributable to a criminal offence. Negligence is irrelevant and it does not matter that the assailant cannot be traced. Awards are made by a specially created body, the Criminal Injuries Compensation Board. This scheme has worked well and has undoubtedly filled a great gap in our compensation schemes.

The success of these schemes has naturally led to pressure for much more widespread reform. The Lord Chief Justice, Lord Parker, has supported this pressure. The argument follows these lines. Take road accidents. We all run the risk of being injured in one. Then we need medical and hospital treatment and perhaps rehabilitation, so that we can get back to work as soon as possible. If we lose our wages we need cash quickly to meet our pressing needs. In other parts of the world, Saskatchewan for instance, schemes providing for payment although there is no negligence have functioned smoothly for years. Why should we get nothing unless we prove negligence, and those fortunate few who do prove it have damages not only for lost earnings, but also further sums for pain and suffering, lost expectation of happiness, lost amenities, loss of limbs and functions? Convince a judge of fault and you might get as much as £50,000 in a lump sum – admittedly some years after the accident; fail to prove fault and you get nothing except a bill for legal costs of both parties, which might well be around £1,000.

Admiring glances are rightly cast at our industrial injury schemes. Could we not similarly take claims by road users away from the courts altogether and replace private insurance by state insurance? Cut down the unnecessary overheads of the present system, so that as much as possible of the accident fund reaches the pockets of the injured, and when they require it most. Give traffic casualties a claim before administrative tribunals like those for industrial injuries. Do not have negligence as the criterion, make the issue simply whether the harm was suffered in consequence of a traffic accident, and have medical matters determined by medical boards and appeal tribunals.[1]

There are of course difficulties in extending this new approach to road traffic. Are passengers to be covered, and, if so, how do you eliminate faked accidents with collusion between driver and passengers? Will the scheme apply to accidents in car parks and hotel drives, or to the mother who suffers nervous shock when her child is hit? What if the victim brought about his injuries by his own recklessness? What is the fair balance between adequate compensation and a scheme which is not too costly? Is there to be compensation for pain, for not being able to play tennis, for loss of the sense of smell? Are high income earners like the Beatles to be paid in full for lost earnings? Is the motorist to bear all the cost, and how is his contribution to be levied? Is the existing common-law action to be retained against the negligent motorist?

Some reformers have more ambitious ideas. They say that it is irrational to remove accident cases from the courts piecemeal. They see no merit in trying out these new proposals in selected areas like road accidents as a prelude to more extensive developments. They point out that more Britishers die and are injured by accidents in the home, for instance, than on the roads. They look to the general trend towards social security plans, and the success of those we have, and propose comprehensive systems of injury compensation.

Developments in New Zealand are interesting. In 1966 the Government set up a Royal Commission to inquire into the law relating to accidents at work. This body, chaired by a Supreme Court judge, concluded that it could not isolate the legal problems relating to industrial accidents. In its Report,

[1]For a detailed treatment of these proposals see D. W. Elliott and Harry Street, *Road Accidents*, Penguin Books, 1968.

published a few months ago,[1] it recommended a social insurance scheme which provided immediate compensation without proof of negligence for any injured person, regardless of his or her fault, and whether the accident occurred in the factory, on the highway or in the home.

The New Zealand proposal discarded the common-law remedy for negligence for much the same reasons as I have talked about earlier. The national interest demands that the community must protect everybody, including housewives, from the burden of sudden individual losses when their productive work is interrupted by physical incapacity caused by accidents. It therefore recommended that everybody be compensated by income-related benefits all the time that they have to be off work; eighty per cent of lost earnings would be paid, with a ceiling of forty to sixty New Zealand pounds a week. The permanently disabled would have additional weekly payments. A government agency would operate the scheme as a social service; insurance companies would play no part. Newly constituted administrative tribunals, not the courts, would hear appeals on claims from the government agency. Proceedings would be speedy and informal. Funds would be furnished by employers contributing one per cent of wages paid out, and by imposing an annual levy on the driving licences of all motorists. The New Zealand Parliament has not yet acted on these recommendations.

At about the same time, Terence Ison, an English barrister who is now a Canadian law professor, published a book[2] which advocates reforms like the New Zealand proposals. He also would abolish actions for personal injuries and replace them by a comprehensive plan of injury compensation. So far as possible the activity which caused the loss would bear the expense, so that he would impose a charge on the use of vehicles through petrol tax and tax employers for industrial accidents. General taxes would meet the balance. There would be income-related

[1]Report of the Royal Commission on Compensation for Personal Injury in New Zealand (1967).

[2]T. Ison, *The Forensic Lottery*, 1968, Staples Press.

periodical payments for loss of earnings, supplemented by lump-sum payments for loss of faculty or disfigurement. He would use the existing national insurance tribunals, not the courts, to decide claims. He maintains that his scheme would involve no extra expenditure, when one takes into account all the insurance premiums paid now to cover possible claims under the existing negligence system.

What are we to make of these proposals? They reflect deep dissatisfaction with the handling by the courts of accident claims. The common-law system is out of tune with current views on community responsibility for injuries which result in loss of production. The big question mark is against the cost of such schemes. We simply have not got the statistical data on which to base reliable judgements – only the Government could procure the figures. All the other difficulties – problems of demarcation, the limits of the scheme, collection of contributions, and allocation of benefits, are surely technical and not insurmountable.

The courts do not seem likely to improve their treatment of accident victims in a way which will meet the serious criticisms levelled at the present law. The Government may now have to examine thoroughly proposals for removing accident cases from the courts.

COULD THE LEGAL SYSTEM BE MORE HUMANE?

Andrew Watson

ZANDER Like many others in our culture, lawyers are today still suspicious of the psychological disciplines. Occasionally this distrust comes out in dramatic form. On one recent occasion, for instance, a judge of the Court of Appeal – during a hearing on the custody of children – said that in the days of his youth psychiatrists had not been invented and no one was any the worse for it. He added for good measure that the psychiatrist appearing for his client was simply a paid advocate – a gibe that would equally apply to any expert witness but which was no doubt provoked by the particular feelings surrounding the psychiatrist. The psychiatrist in that particular case felt so insulted that he got up and walked out of court. This kind of attitude on the part of the judges is fortunately now less common, but we are still a long way from a full appreciation that psychological insights could make a real and practical contribution to the improvement of the law and the legal system. The Americans are in this respect far in advance of us. There is nothing in this country comparable to the position held by psychiatrists or psychoanalysts in several leading American law schools. What is even more striking is that they are employed there to teach not simply their own subjects but law. Professor Andrew Watson is an American psychiatrist and psychoanalyst who for years has been teaching criminal law and family law to law students. He has also spent some time in this country studying our legal system. He is therefore particularly well placed to talk about a problem of concern both to lawyers and laymen and which has been referred to by several speakers in this series – whether the legal system is sufficiently humane.

WATSON To explore the question of humaneness in the law

presents a fine challenge to a social psychiatrist. It requires the analysis of a social institution which deals with issues of morality and authority, and which engages the intellectual and emotional involvement of lay clients with professional lawyers and judges. Every aspect of this complicated situation lends itself to psychological scrutiny.

The lawyer with his concern for legal abstractions such as Justice, Liberty of the Subject, Equity, as well as a multitude of others, by necessity sets himself at some distance apart from personal considerations. The rule of law and concepts like the doctrine of precedent, which provide stability and a reasonable predictability to the law, by their very nature tend toward human remoteness. At the same time, it is vital that the members of society governed by the rule of law have a deep conviction that the issues brought to law will be disposed of with justice. In Britain you have a lovely way of putting this which demonstrates high awareness of the emotional aspects of the problem. You say that 'not only must justice be done, but it must appear to have been done'. This pays close attention to the public's concerns and attitudes.

Laws and legal procedures by their very nature are so technically complex that, at best, laymen can only grope for their meanings. This of course is a characteristic of the work of all professionals. The professional person owes a special duty to make the client's best interests his primary concern, particularly because his professional activities are to a great extent performed behind the scenes, out of sight of the client, who is normally unable to evaluate the quality of the work done. But the professional lawyer also has a duty as a member of the legal profession to further client interests only within the limits of the law. We see at once that this produces a potential conflict of interests with the inevitable result that it may create emotional tension for both the client and the lawyer. An example of this occurs in a criminal trial where defence counsel may and should use every legitimate defence tactic for his client, though he is under an obligation as a member of the profession to avoid obstructing legitimate prosecution procedures. If this tension is not dealt with, the predictable result will be that the client will feel he has been dealt with unjustly, and the lawyer will feel he has not done his job well. A successful lawyer must therefore possess the psychological skill to help his clients resolve such tensions. Whether he be solicitor, barrister, or judge, it should be a matter of professional duty to make at least an attempt to do this. What tools do lawyers possess at the present time to carry out this difficult task?

In Britain and for the most part in the United States, it is sheer chance if counsel possesses these skills. We cannot readily blame them, however, for there is nothing in the formal training of lawyers to develop their potential capacity to deal with the psychological aspects of law practice. While great lawyers have this skill to an impressive degree, the vast majority seem to lack even what might be called common-sense awareness of their clients' emotions. This I attribute to a negative effect of legal education, as well as partially to the personality traits in those who choose to practise law. Lawyers are taught and urged to distrust and to eliminate emotions from their work. As if this were possible! They might as well attempt to fly with their hands!

In Britain, the division of the legal profession into barristers and solicitors provides an interesting potential for helping clients to understand and express themselves freely about what has happened in the course of their contacts with the law. When an issue goes to trial, the aloof and intellectual barrister will carry out his function of advocacy according to law, insulated as it were from the client. He can fulfil the community-oriented objectives of the law, leaving the task of restoring the equanimity and understanding of the litigants to the solicitors. This has the effect of forcing the solicitor to be a kind of diplomat-conciliator. His effectiveness in the community depends on his carrying this out, and his self-interest in keeping his clients happy provides the guarantee that he will do so. I have also gained the impression that the frequently differing social backgrounds of solicitors and barristers tends to fit them to carry out these different roles. Solicitors seem to be drawn from a sector of the community which makes them a bit more able to identify with, and be responsive to, the personal concerns of their clients. On the other hand, barristers, generally educated at the older universities and drawn from families more familiar with abstract social concerns, quite naturally fit into the more formal atmosphere of courtroom pleading and consultative work. This division of labour facilitates a deliberate approach to the dual task of helping the community understand the law, at the same time as the rule of law is maintained in relatively remote, but logical verbal abstractions. The two kinds of lawyers can carry out these different goals. If at some future time the profession should alter its present structure, for example by unifying its two branches, these distinct functions will still need to be handled and their importance recognised by appropriate training measures.

Of course we must acknowledge that most Englishmen's experience with the law takes place in the magistrates' courts and the county courts. Here there is less of the magical aura cast by the professional lawyers than in the higher courts. In fact, litigants in the magistrates' court are usually not represented at all. The atmosphere there is more informal. There seems to be a recent trend also of appointing members of the magistrates' bench from a broader spectrum of society, which should improve the rapport between the community and the law. This is a commendable trend. Nothing better improves community acceptance and understanding of the law than the reality of involvement, as for example in the obligation to serve on a jury. I might note in passing that such involvement in community activities is, to me, one of the impressive characteristics of British society.

Another aspect of British legal procedure, which is psychologically important and which deserves extension and emulation, is the concept of making most of the elements used in the court's decision-making highly visible to the observer. Everything the judge uses and considers is heard in open court. There are no written arguments for judges to evaluate in private.

This promotes community participation and evaluation,

even though not as extensively as one would wish. This effect could be heightened through further clarification of some of the more abstruse legal issues as they arise in the courtroom. Thus judges might view themselves as having an educative role as well as being interpreters of the law. The distance between interpretation and education is small. Ways should be found for making their views on important public matters more widely known. Today's communication media should make wide dissemination of important decisions a relatively simple task.

I suppose one would have to say that, to most of the community, law and lawyers are viewed as being related to matters Olympian, or as contemporary remnants of a society dominated by the upper classes. Most laymen do not fully or even partially understand the well-tuned beauty of legal processes and the way in which they protect the hard-earned cultural gains of a society. They do not appreciate the subtle checks and balances of legal procedures, which make law the relatively effective social instrument it is, notwithstanding a multitude of deficiencies. Rather it is seen as a mysterious and threatening apparatus, ever hovering just out of sight, ready to envelop and punish one for real or imagined misconduct. It speaks with Jovian wrath, ready to smite Evil and uphold Good. Such imagery is similar to the imagery of a child's conscience and, as such, it works to impede the rational development of the law both in terms of public acceptance as well as in the behaviour of many who work in the legal profession. It is just this kind of imagery which stands in antithesis to a humane legal system.

In primitive as well as relatively recent legal systems, the principle of an eye for an eye, tooth for a tooth, was viewed as just. Even today, when we are greatly frightened by some heinous crime, such as the Shepherd's Bush shooting of three constables in 1967, there is an immediate impulse to revive the death penalty and other severe punishments. This response is 'explained' as an effort to deter those vicious characters among us who would commit such crimes. In our more rational moments, however, we can often recognise such retributive impulses as merely the biological responses to fear. They do not prevent such crimes and indeed many people realise that persons who commit such violent acts seem to have something grossly wrong with them. This kind of awareness on a broad social scale has gradually produced the feeling and belief that, to punish, there must be evidence of a guilty state of mind, what lawyers call *mens rea*. The introduction of this idea into the law has been a step in the humanising of the law. It is closely akin to the moral belief of turning the other cheek and it reflects a stage in the evolution of a humane law and a humanistic society. In other words humaneness includes the psychological need to understand *why* a crime is committed and it reflects a trend in society's belief that only those who freely *choose* to behave criminally should be subjected to a retributive counter-assault by society. This evolving awareness of the nature of man's inner psychological behaviour and its relationship to social control brings in its wake a conflict between the biological attribute of self-protective vengeance and the social insights that there are some whom punishment will not deter, and that carrying out punishment on them often makes the punisher feel bad. This conflict lies at the heart of a multitude of social and legal problems, which may be resolved rationally only through application of the insights of modern psychological and social theories.

The most direct way this might be done is to transport some of this knowledge about human behaviour into the training of lawyers. It is ironical and even deplorable that those who have so much to do with the shaping of law and legal institutions have so little formal contact with this knowledge. It is tantamount to training an engineer without the use of mathematics, yet this is what is done in most countries. Ideally, every lawyer's education should include at least a grounding in human psychology. He should learn what we know about interviewing skills. What happens when a client sits down with an authority figure such as his lawyer? What are the psychological forces which operate between the parties to such a conversation, that may obscure issues and produce failures of communication? How can a sensitive interviewer avoid these risks or dispel them when they exist? The answer to such questions is to be found in the substance of the psychological sciences and before long we should view it as a matter of neglect if they are not included in the routine training of all lawyers.

Another place where modern psychological knowledge could and should be used to make law more humane is in relation to the procedures of the law. For example, we know that a person confronted with the massive power of the state may do things that appear suspicious or as evidence of guilt, even when he has done no wrong. Concern about psychological reactions to such situations would help to promote interest in ways of avoiding or at least minimising the danger that the system may make mistakes because of such misleading behaviour. This is especially worrisome in criminal cases. The legal rules protecting defendants against self-incrimination were intuitive responses developed by the common law hundreds of years ago to take account of the psychological phenomena. We are now in a position to improve upon these procedural rules, to increase the level of understanding of what is going on in legal proceedings, civil as well as criminal.

Another sort of use for psychological knowledge in legal procedures may be seen in relation to such questions as eye-witness reliability. The widely accepted hunch that emotions can seriously distort the accuracy of eye-witness evidence has now been scientifically proved. Such data should be used to improve the efficiency of legal fact-finding. A need to believe in the accuracy of the facts used in legal procedures is not only connected with the community's sense of justice, it promotes humaneness as well.

Under present rules of procedure, the parties to an action are ordinarily the passive recipients of the results. Often they are left with many unsettled questions, and indeed delusions, as to what happened to them in court. It should always be borne in mind that it is relatively unimportant that the lawyers believe that everything has been clarified and settled, if the parties do not. So far as they are concerned, the matter has not been justly handled. Means must be found for using the formidable power and authority of the court setting to improve and facilitate the communication between the litigating parties. While such changes might prolong the proceedings somewhat, the overall social efficiency would be greatly increased. Such considerations as this are another example of how psychological knowledge about people might be used to make the proceedings and imagery of the law more humane.

I have been much impressed with the image of dignity and justice which is present in the British High Court. Even the wigs and robes foster this. However, side by side there is often a kind of icy aloofness which does not foster effective communication. We now know a great deal about the effects of gestures, voice inflection, and body postures on communication. In fact, such non-verbal means of communication are probably at least as important as the words used. It should be possible for judges to learn this new knowledge about the processes of communication, as well as how their own personalities affect the ease of witnesses, the impact of their words on juries, and their effectiveness in communication generally. This could help to make clear that they are humanely in touch with the people before them. Some judges already have this proficiency and it does not appear to erode their judicial authority or objectiveness. Perhaps ways can be found for fostering changes in this direction, through such means as the recent development, both in America and in this country, of judicial training conferences. Surely it is not disrespectful to suggest that there are some special skills needed by judges which they will not automatically have gained through their previous work as barristers.

Finally the legal profession should utilise its prestige to educate the public in the ways of justice. As I remarked earlier, few laymen understand the nature of the judicial process. They will give away valuable liberties by inadvertance and ignorance, even as they believe that they are making gains for their own security. I would say that lawyers are the possessors of some very heady and exciting knowledge. They should make a greater effort to help us know what they are doing and how they do it. Some few have already done this in books, plays and public lectures, but it is far from enough. With all the capability of modern communications media, lawyers should share the excitement of their concerns with us. Let us see, too, how deeply concerned they are with our welfare. This will automatically make the law more humane, because it will make it more understandable.

One of the psychological paradoxes about the law is that in all our society there is no other group more concerned than lawyers about basic human values. Yet because of the technical complexity which surrounds it, this concern all too often remains largely invisible to the public. Thus lawyers and judges do not get full credit for their efforts and are widely misunderstood. May I suggest that we would all benefit from vigorous attention to this matter by the legal profession. We the public would feel more secure with our legal institutions, while the members of the legal profession would receive the satisfying reward of public admiration in return for their efforts.

WHO IS AT FAULT WHEN INJUSTICE OCCURS?

LORD DEVLIN

ZANDER That great lawyer Reginald Heber Smith once said:

> Nothing rankles more in the human heart than a brooding sense of injustice. Illness we can put up with; but injustice makes us want to pull things down.

This feeling is shared by lawyer and layman alike – but with one important difference. The layman is usually concerned first with justice in the individual case. He believes that law and justice should be synonymous and is angry and impatient with the lawyers when the legal system perpetrates what appears to him to be injustice. The lawyer, whilst anxious to do justice in the individual case, thinks that the maximum of justice is created by rules and procedures which are general and uniform in their application. The lawyer strives therefore not for justice plain and simple. This seems to him to be too personalised and subjective to be reliable. Instead he looks for justice according to law and accepts that this will sometimes mean injustice according to law. The tension between the desire for justice in individual cases and the necessity of seeking it through the law is inevitable in any legal system. Yet systems obviously vary in the extent to which they succeed in achieving justice. In some extreme cases, like that of Nazi Germany, justice through law becomes a mere mockery. But even in liberal and tolerant regimes there is always the danger that the rigidity of technical rules or the narrowness of judicial attitudes or the creakiness of the machinery of reform may cause more injustice than is necessary. Even the best systems fall far short of the ideal of justice. In the last of this series of talks, Lord Devlin gives his view of how much injustice can be said to exist in our system and to what extent one can identify who or what is responsible.

DEVLIN One cannot measure the extent of injustice without distinguishing between criminal and civil law. Not only is our criminal administration quite different from civil and our criminal law much more complete, but in seeking to do justice in criminal matters we do not put the prosecution and the defence on the same level. Indeed, we often do an injustice to the prosecution so as to ensure as far as we can that none is done to the accused. I cannot in a brief space cover both criminal and civil, and so I shall take civil only, since it is the law's deficiencies in securing for the citizen his just rights that have been the main subject of these talks.

Injustice for this purpose means something stronger than an error of judgement which produces a wrong result. Justice is not infallible. Every judge has had the experience of trying a case where the result depends entirely on whether he believes the plaintiff or the defendant. A judge would have to be a very self-satisfied person if, looking back on these sort of cases in his past, he was quite confident that he had got the answer right every time. Provided that he has been given a fair trial and that the judge has been seen to be careful and impartial, a plaintiff who has been wrongly disbelieved, painful though it may be, ought not to feel that he has been the victim of injustice.

Further I regard 'injustice' as meaning more than the hard case that can from time to time be produced by the straightforward application of the law. The object of a rule is to ensure that similar cases are similarly decided; if they were not, then there would not be justice at all. Michael Zander has already made the point that any rule, however well phrased, may occasionally interfere with judgement on the merits. Justice for all carries with it the possibility of something less than justice in the individual case.

If I am not right in interpreting injustice in this way, then the answer to the question must be that quite often when it occurs, it is nobody's fault. So I shall treat it as meaning something in the nature of a miscarriage of justice, something that could have been prevented if the system were better designed and the men who worked it more competent.

Let us take the men first. The judge must be an upright, intelligent and independent man. And since intelligence can sometimes falter and the single judge can have his off days, there must be some right of appeal as a safeguard. Not much complaint is heard today about the quality of our judges. The review of a case that is conducted by the Court of Appeal – particularly an appeal from the High Court when a transcript of all the evidence is available – is a very thorough one. I should say that the chance of injustice occurring because of judicial defects is small.

But any decision, however good the decision-maker may be, will be wrong if it is made on incorrect or inadequate information. Under our system it is the responsibility of the advocate – I use that term to cover both barrister and solicitor – the advocate on each side to see that all the relevant facts are brought before the judge. This is what is known as the adversary system as opposed to the inquisitorial. When for example a government inquiry is set up to investigate, let us say, the causes of a national disaster, there is no opposition of adversaries and the commission of inquiry has to be armed with powers to ascertain the facts for itself. Under the adversary system it is presumed that if each side produces the evidence in its own favour, the judge will at the end of the day have the whole picture in front of him. Indeed, I think myself that he will get a better picture that way than if he does the job himself, provided of course that the advocates are competent.

You observe that I talk about competent advocacy rather than good or bad advocacy. Ought I not, you may ask, to consider the possibility of injustice arising through bad advocates losing cases they ought to win and good advocates winning cases they ought to lose? I do not think so. In a short talk I must leave out of account jury cases which nowadays form only a tiny proportion of civil litigation. The good advocate nowadays is no longer the orator with the golden voice but the man who knows how to present facts and argument audibly and clearly. But an advocate who cannot do even that is on the whole unlikely to lose his case because of it, though he will certainly give the judge more trouble. Of course the easier the judge's task is made in these respects the more likely he is to arrive at the correct judgement. But I doubt if bad advocacy in this sense is a substantial cause of injustice. It is a matter of balance. High quality output from the advocate will compensate for a low-powered intake of the judge and vice versa. It is unfortunate when low output meets with low intake but the deleterious effects of the combination do not usually survive the Court of Appeal.

If we pass the system as adequate and the men who have to administer it as competent, what is left to criticise? Only the law that they have to administer. And this series has been largely devoted to trying to find out what is wrong with the law. What I now have to consider is to what extent bad law is actually a source of injustice.

Here one must distinguish. A law can be bad because its content is bad. Except in so far as he can use his knowledge of the way the law works to suggest improvements, a lawyer can do no more about this than the ordinary citizen. If an Act of Parliament which is clear and precise results in injustice, there is nothing to be done with it except repeal it and that is not the job of the lawyer as such. For the lawyer as such a bad law is one that does not state clearly what it wants the judge to do. That is why these talks have been concerned so much with the obscurity of the law. Obviously there is a waste of money if the elucidation of the law takes longer than is necessary. But estimating obscurity as a direct source of injustice I should say that, while appreciable, it is not enormous. The fact is that only a tiny minority of cases turn upon a disputed point of law. Every now and again a judge says with sorrow that the law prevents him from doing what he believes to be just, but statistically such cases are rare.

Can we then conclude comfortably that in England there is very little injustice? I am afraid not. Where injustice is to be found is not so much in the cases that come to court, but in those that are never brought there. The main field of injustice is not litigation but non-litigation, and the prime cause of non-litigation is twofold: first, the incompleteness and obscurity of the law that prevents or deters action, and secondly the appalling cost. The two together have turned litigation, which ought to be a gentle solvent of disputes, into a thing of horror.

Now as to the first, Mr Justice Scarman has already talked about obscurity, and so I shall say a word about incompleteness. The law cannot provide a remedy for every sort of misbehaviour. But I think that as between citizens, and also as between the citizen and the state, English law leaves far too many serious grievances without redress.

The law that deals with misbehaviour of one citizen towards another is the law of torts. A tort is a civil wrong causing injury. Most countries have a code of civil law whose framers have surveyed the whole field of misbehaviour, decided what the law can remedy and what it cannot, and composed the code accordingly. Not so in England. In the centuries in which the law of torts was being formulated, a plaintiff brought his grievance to a court of law and the court decided whether or not it was a tort. The process of creation, at first potent, became weaker as the centuries went by. The creation of a new tort is now very rare and takes a very long time. It is rather like the process of canonisation. The cause is first of all fostered by academic wellwishers and then promoted in the lower courts. Eventually, if things prosper, the tort will be beatified by the Court of Appeal and then, probably after a long interval, it will achieve full sainthood in the House of Lords. The tort of intimidation, for example, which for at least a century had been wandering about in the textbooks in an unblessed state, was sanctified by the House of Lords in 1964.[1] Naturally under these conditions the growth of the law has been lopsided.

But if as between individuals the law does something but not enough, where the individual has a grievance against the bureaucracy the law does virtually nothing. Government servants can of course commit torts and when they do the law gives them no immunity. But the power of government, national and local, is now such that the citizen can be injured in innumerable

[1]In *Rookes v. Barnard* [1964] A.C. 1129.

ways by acts of maladministration. Mr Warren Evans dealt with this in his talk. Most civilised countries now feel the need of what is called administrative law to protect the citizen against the state, but we have little or none.

Now what about expense? It is generally agreed that for the ordinary citizen the cost of litigation is prohibitive. What is the reason? I do not believe it is on the whole because lawyers take extortionate fees; the average lawyer is no richer than the average member of other professions. Some people think that the duplication of work between barrister and solicitor puts up the costs. Personally I think that you would save no more money by abolishing the distinction between barristers and solicitors than you would in medicine by abolishing the distinction between specialists and G.P.s; but anyway I am sure that what you saved would not be enough. Various committees have from time to time been appointed to investigate the cost of litigation and they have been able to prune expenditure here and there but never to make any substantial impact. Nor will they so long as they do not dare to tackle the two features of our procedure which truly account for its enormous cost. These are the adversary system and the insistence upon oral evidence. Under the adversary system each side prepares its case in secret, giving away as little as possible to its opponent. In this way the work is trebled, each side conducting an investigation on its own and then the two meeting in confrontation. As for the insistence upon oral evidence, this not only produces a heavy bill for the attendance of witnesses but means, since the judge has to make a note of the evidence, that the pace of the trial proceeds at the speed at which he can write instead of at the speed at which he can read. In an appeal court, where oral presentation is also insisted upon, things are a little faster because they proceed at the speed of talk; and though talking is much slower than reading, it is faster than writing.

In my opinion we shall not make any worthwhile saving in the cost of litigation so long as we accept it as the inalienable right of every litigant to have the whole of his evidence and argument presented by word of mouth. It is not a right that is recognised by any legal system except the English and those that are based on it. In many systems it is left to the court itself to determine to what extent, if at all, a hearing is necessary. We ourselves accept that justice can be done by domestic tribunals without all the setting of the legal trial. Simple cases could, I think, often be solved by the judge alone, perhaps with the aid of an inquiry officer but without the need for professional advocacy. Where that is not feasible the judge should have a complete discretion to decide what form the trial should take. In appellate work the case could be decided on paper – with perhaps a limited hearing for oral argument on any point that the court thought needed elucidation – in a quarter of the time that is now occupied partly by speech but mainly by the reading aloud of documents.

But would the result be absolutely as good? I am not prepared to say that. When a film is played in slow motion detail will be observed that might otherwise be missed. Undoubtedly there are cases in which a part – and perhaps a few in which the greater part – ought to be conducted in slow motion. The art lies in scanning the whole so as to ascertain where detailed development is necessary.

But, it may be said, if time and money are no object, why not be on the safe side and always play the whole in slow motion? Why not? The fallacy inherent in our High Court procedure of civil litigation is just that – that where justice is concerned, time and money are no object. We think of British justice as an ideal into which such sordid considerations ought not to enter. We refuse to associate with it such homely maxims as that half a loaf is better than no bread. But is it right to cling to a system that offers perfection for the few and nothing at all for the many? Perhaps: if we could really be sure that our existing system was perfect. But of course it is not. We delude ourselves if we think that it always produces the right judgement. Every system contains a percentage of error; and if by slightly increasing the percentage of error, we can substantially reduce the percentage of cost, it is only the idealist who will revolt.

Over a century ago we made a deliberate decision to reduce

the standard of justice so as to increase its spread. We instituted the County Court – the poor man's court, as it used to be called. If, as I think must be admitted, standards of justice depend upon the qualities of judge and advocate, we must accept that the County Court aims at a lower standard than the High Court. It cannot be expected always to attract judges of equal ability or advocates of as much experience. And what has since become much more important than either of these factors is that in the County Court, so as to save expense, no transcript is usually taken of the evidence and this inevitably increases the risk of an erroneous judgement of fact going unrectified in the Court of Appeal.

The creation of the County Court was in its time a revolutionary attempt to make justice an economic proposition. We need now to make another attempt of the same magnitude. I may be right or wrong in thinking that we can cut costs drastically by doing more on paper. I think I am right: but what I am sure about is that if we cannot do it that way, we must do it some other way. We must start a search for a new procedure, applying unashamedly the principle that the coat must be cut according to the cloth.

DISCUSSION

Chairman: Michael Zander
Speakers: Lord Devlin
Anthony Lester
Sir Leslie Scarman

ZANDER This series of programmes has explored some of the defects of the law and the legal system. We have looked at the law's complexity and rigidity, at its obscurity, and at its cost. We have examined particular problems such as equality before the law, the relationship between the individual and the state, and the role of the legal profession. Now three of the contributors to the series join me in a discussion of some of the practical problems and priorities of law reform. They are Lord Devlin, Sir Leslie Scarman and Mr Anthony Lester.

One theme that has emerged strongly in the series is the crucial role that will be played by the Law Commission in deciding what needs to be done, and in preparing the necessary draft legislation. But what prospect is there actually that Parliament will find the time to cope with what one imagines will be a steadily increasing flow of legislative proposals. Is this a serious problem, Sir Leslie?

SCARMAN It is already a very serious problem and almost certain to become more so.

ZANDER Do you think in fact that Parliament realises how serious this problem is? Is there any evidence that its techniques or procedures have been adjusted to deal with what one imagines will be an increasing problem?

SCARMAN I am not at all sure that members of either House fully appreciate the size of the problem. I am quite sure that the men and women in charge of the legislative programme, particularly people like the Lord Chancellor, are well aware of it.

ZANDER Lord Devlin, do you see the House of Lords playing any significant role in adjusting the procedures of Parliament to deal with this problem?

DEVLIN Well, only as a stopgap. I mean, the House of Lords is there. It consists of intelligent people. It is underworked with serious business, and it could do what the Commons has not got time to do.

ZANDER How could it do this in practice? What actual contribution could it make?

DEVLIN Just by discussing Bills in the way in which it normally does. I had not visualised it doing anything more than that as a stopgap. If you are going to consider some entirely new and different sort of procedure, then at the same time I would suggest you consider an entirely new and different sort of body, and not the House of Lords.

ZANDER So you do not think that the House of Lords as at present composed could make any particular contribution?

DEVLIN I do not know that Sir Leslie would agree – but I think what you want is some totally different sort of body altogether. Any body with complete legislative power cannot do more really than lay down principles. It has not got time to do anything else. Its people will not be equipped to do anything else. What you need is some sort of a body that will scrutinise the details, some sort of subordinate legislative body. That is what it seems to me has got to be created.

SCARMAN I agree with Lord Devlin. What are needed are new legislative techniques. These techniques cannot themselves be implemented by either the House of Commons or the House of Lords. Those two bodies, which will no doubt remain sovereign in the field of legislation, have got to create machinery ancillary to themselves to prepare and take the controversy out of much of the legislative programme. One of the things one learns in the Law Commission is the needless controversy over legislation in the two Houses. There is always bound to be controversy, but very few Bills contain more than one or two points of genuine controversy. The trouble about legislation is that it is clothed by our system in unnecessary controversy. Controversy must remain, but let us keep it concentrated on the issues that are really controversial.

ZANDER But how can one go about this process of first reducing the controversy to the essential, presumably political, elements, and secondly giving the draft legislation that will come out of the proposals of the Law Commission the necessary scrutiny which I imagine you accept is still necessary, even after the Law Commission has had its say?

SCARMAN I see the Law Commission as primarily and fundamentally a research and advisory body standing a little apart from the machinery of government or the machinery of legislation. What is needed is a development of techniques in two spheres of governmental activity. First of all, on the executive side, there ought to be a department of state, organised on a much grander scale than, for instance, the Lord Chancellor's department, which will give to legislative proposals scrutiny in their pre-Parliamentary stage. Then the two legislative bodies – Lords and Commons – need to develop either a committee structure or some other structure which would itself look at legislation, after it has been through the executive sieve and before it reaches the floor of either House. If you do that, and if those bodies erected either by government or by legislature, had the benefit of the advice of the Law Commission, you will be on the way to a scientific process of legislation.

ZANDER Does this mean that one is moving towards a Ministry of Justice?

SCARMAN Well if you ask me that, Mr Zander, I should say I hope so.

ZANDER Lord Devlin, there has been a traditional reluctance to accept the idea of a Ministry of Justice in this country. Can you identify the causes of this reluctance?

DEVLIN I should think just good, honest, traditional reluctance.

Personally I feel a traditional reluctance to any sort of new ministry and a traditional clinging to the old ways in which we have done things, but I think that Sir Leslie has just epitomised a very strong case. It is not so much a Ministry of Justice as opposed to a Lord Chancellor: it is much more that there must be a larger department of state than the Lord Chancellor controls. I should think that the Minister must be in the Commons. And then added to that, once you get those conditions the Lord Chancellor could no longer combine certain traditional duties, of presiding over the House of Lords for instance, with the result that it does seem to me inevitably to lead to a Ministry of Justice.

ZANDER But there does seem to be a feeling that a Ministry of Justice is incompatible with the freedom of the individual, particularly in relation to the state. Do you feel that there is anything in this, Anthony Lester?

LESTER No, I do not. I agree with what has been said, that we need a Ministry of Justice. The fear arises partly because the Lord Chancellor is the Minister who appoints judges, and it has always been felt that there should not be too close a link between politicians and the bench – otherwise the independence of the judiciary may be undermined. There is that fear. There are also, I think, misconceptions about those other systems of law, especially on the continent, in which there are Ministers of Justice. The fear of authoritarian systems of law is based on misconceptions going back to Dicey, but I see no reason at all why having a politician in the Cabinet and in the House of Commons in charge of a Ministry of Justice should undermine the independence of the bench at all.

DEVLIN I think things like the appointment of judges, power to appoint judges, would require very careful consideration. Obviously there would be other things as well, but one can only say in the very broadest way that a Ministry of Justice is a good thing.

ZANDER If one has a Ministry of Justice, the Law Commission would engage on a study of a particular topic and would come out at the end, having consulted with all the relevant interests, both legal and extra-legal, with draft legislation. Now supposing the Minister of Justice took a completely different view and thought that the Law Commission was on the wrong lines, or supposing that the Ministry of Justice put it forward but Parliament then amended it in all sorts of ways without reference to the consultations which the Law Commission had gone through, at great length and with great care, would this be a mistake?

SCARMAN I do not think it would be a mistake, because I agree with Anthony Lester on the importance of retaining Parliamentary control over legislation and I think it is extremely important that the techniques that Lord Devlin and I were describing as possible a few moments ago should be seen as subordinate to Parliament, as assisting Parliament and not superseding Parliament. You raise, Mr Zander, two points, and I can deal with them quite shortly. First of all, what ought to happen if a Minister of Justice receives from the Law Commission law-reform proposals with which he disagrees. First, he should of course be obliged to publish them, so that people can see what is being proposed and rejected in the field of law reform; but secondly, he must retain his right as a member of the Government, and it is the duty of the Government to govern – to say we will legislate this way, and not that way. The legislative programme of the Government must be for the Government itself to choose, and if they choose not to put forward certain law-reform proposals, whether they emanate from the Law Commission or elsewhere, they must be within their rights, and I think this is necessary to sound government. Your second question was what happens if law-reform proposals that have been carefully considered by a body like the Law Commission get hopelessly, and in a most disfiguring way, amended in Parliament. Again I would recognise and support the right of Parliament to impose what amendments it thinks fit upon proposals, however carefully considered and emanating from however expert a body. That does not mean to say that I want to see law reform disfigured by amendments, but the right to amend must be there.

DEVLIN What I should like to see – but perhaps it is totally impractical – is some sort of tidying up process at the end. I absolutely agree with Sir Leslie – you must have the power to amend, and if its preservation results in an untidy piece of legislation, that is part of our liberties. But is there any way in which one could introduce a tidying up process by going back to the Law Commission?

SCARMAN Yes, Lord Devlin, undoubtedly there is. It will be necessary, I have no doubt, to improve the means of communication between a body like the Law Commission and the legislative bodies like the two Houses of Parliament. Already members of the legal staff of the Law Commission attend in the so-called 'box' when legislation emanating from the Law Commission is going through the House of Commons or the House of Lords. They are there to assist whoever is responsible for the passage of the Bill in dealing with amendments or in proposing and drafting amendments emanating from the government side. Clearly if one has a big piece of law-reform legislation, like for instance the Contract Code or Criminal Law Code, going through the House, and an amendment is made which appears to undermine certain principles upon which the Code is based, then it must go back to the Law Commission for study and for further formulation in the light of the amendment. I see no difficulties in the matter of machinery in ensuring the assistance of the Law Commission during the legislative process, just as we already now have it before the legislative process.

LESTER Could I just add to that? I think that two ways in which one could prevent bad amendments being made to technical Bills, or to Bills dealing with law reform, would first be by having earlier publication of the principles on which a Bill is to be based and more open debate before the Bill itself is published. I am sure that the notion of a Select Committee which can take evidence, and educate and inform itself, and publish reports on desirable law-reform legislation in collaboration with the Law Commission is one way of making sure that the principles are understood before the Bill is drafted. The second point is that I think that most of the worst cases of illogical or bad amendments occur at the committee stage in the legislative process. And therefore if one could have some convention whereby members of the Select Committee who are dealing all the time with law reform could form a substantial part of members dealing with the committee stage of a Bill, one would avoid a lot of nonsense at that stage.

SCARMAN I agree with you on that. In fact if you have Law Commission staff members attending, as they now do, for the committee stage of Bills which emanate from the Law Commission, the risk of bad amendments is largely reduced.

ZANDER What about the relatively recent development of specialist parliamentary committees looking into things like privacy or race relations? Is this a helpful innovation in parliamentary procedure in terms of law reform? Anthony Lester, you have been following the race relations committee.

LESTER It is too early to tell what is going to happen, because the new legislation on that subject is only a matter of three or four months old. But I have just been reading the evidence given to the Select Committee on Race Relations, and I am absolutely sure that the Members of Parliament who have served on it will be much better informed and be better able to evaluate the legislation as a result of the work that they have done. It may be that as a result of that work they will decide that the legislation needs to be amended. If that does happen I would hope that those Members of Parliament play a key role in the crucial committee stage that any future Bill will have to go through.

DEVLIN But the difficulty in looking at it as a piece of machinery is this, is it not – that Members of Parliament simply have not got the time to be specialists? It is highly desirable, of course, if they do it in one particular thing, but there are many, many other things that they have to deal with. They could not really be specialists in all the topics they have got to deal with, or even any reasonable number of them. I would think that when you are looking at the sort of machinery you want it is better to keep Members of Parliament occupied for the actual pushing through of legislation, and let what you might call the research and specialist work be done by other bodies and brought up to them.

LESTER Well, I think it is also important, though, that they should continually be re-educating themselves about legislation. It may be one needs – and this is going rather wide of our subject – special legislative aides, as they have in the United States, to help Members of Parliament to understand legislation and the technicalities of legal drafting. But I think it would be dangerous to allow specialist bodies outside Parliament to have the main responsibility for scrutinising legislation, and then to have, as it were, without using too patronising a term – to educate Members of Parliament who are out of touch with the content of legislation. I think that at the moment the tendency is for Members of Parliament to become increasingly professional and full-time, and to spend two or three mornings a week in committee.

SCARMAN I think there is value in specialist parliamentary committees, but I would like you to consider the value to be attached to committees drawn from *both* Houses. You will find specialists in the House of Lords, just as you will find specialists in the House of Commons. And a Joint Select Committee of the two Houses can be of real assistance in the field of law reform in, so to speak, siphoning out controversy from measures which, if properly understood, should not really give rise to controversy, save perhaps on one or two points. You probably know about the Consolidation and Statute Law Revision Joint Select Committee. This does a magnificent job of work in a very technical field and I should have thought similar committees dealing with similar technical questions of law could possibly be developed in regard to other legislation.

ZANDER Do you see this, though, as something which will be in addition to work already done by the Law Commission, or on fields which have not yet been touched by the specialist law-reform body?

SCARMAN Well, speaking for myself, very much working upon measures that have themselves emanated from the Law Commission, which will have done the research and will have gone through the processes of consultation necessary for sound law reform.

ZANDER This seems to me an important point – that you, as Chairman of the Law Commission, hope that the Law Commission will be, as it were, the engine room of law reform, initiating measures and also deciding to a great extent who does what, rather than the previous method of law reform where everybody did a little bit and there was no central guidance or direction.

SCARMAN This is my credo as Chairman of the Law Commission, and I have the support of Section 3 of the Law Commission's Act 1965.[1]

ZANDER Can I just draw out one general point which has, I think, emerged from various things that have been said – namely, the idea that there is something called technical law reform as opposed to other kinds of law reform which are not perhaps law reform at all. I think there is a certain division of opinion, amongst lawyers at least. Lord Devlin, do you believe that technical law reform can be distinguished from other kinds of law reform?

DEVLIN I think that at one end of law reform you have technical questions, and at another end you have sociological questions. And so if a particular question belongs to one extreme or the other you can say that it is technical or sociological. But they tend to merge so much in the middle that I do not think you could ever make a useful division for the purpose of devising some new sort of machinery.

[1]Section 3 sets out the functions of the Law Commissions including the duty 'to take and keep under review all the law with which they are respectively concerned with a view to its systematic development and reform . . .'

ZANDER Is this a division that ought really to be made for the purposes of, say, initiation of legislation by the Law Commission? The Law Commission, I think, is seen by many as being concerned primarily with technical problems, lawyers' problems, rather than social-economic problems. Is this how the Commission sees its own role?

SCARMAN No, not at all. The term 'lawyers' law' has no relevance to law reform as I understand it. It originates from a consideration of the sort of legal topics which engage the attention of solicitors and barristers in private practice. These are only a small percentage of the legal topics of importance to the community. There are vast ranges of the statute law dealing with, for instance, the whole social security system, which strictly fall outside the term 'lawyers' law' and yet are just as technical and just as difficult as any point that you can identify as lawyers' law. It is a term which I dislike and I hope will disappear into oblivion. There are some fields of law which are more technical than others and naturally, the Law Commission is supposed to possess the expertise to understand and handle technical questions of law. But, in my four years at the Law Commission, I have never yet found a problem of law reform that was worth doing anything about which did not have an important social element. I agree with Lord Devlin that the social element varies according to subject-matter, but it is always there. And it is because of the existence of that social element that law reform should never be entrusted to lawyers alone. If you do entrust it to lawyers, those lawyers, through a process of consultation and publication, must bring the public into the job.

LESTER I enthusiastically agree with what Sir Leslie has just said. There is a great danger in seeing any question of law reform as a linguistic or verbal or technical question. The English legal system seems to me already to suffer from an undue preoccupation with linguistics, with questions of language, with interpretation, and with insulation from the social context of law. And it seems to me vital, if we are embarking on a new period of law reform with new machinery, that we should see the law as far as we can in its social context, while recognising that there may well be some areas of law where the social context is relatively limited.

ZANDER One of the features of law reform in certain key areas with very important social overtones over the last few years has been the part played by the private member in Parliament, in fields such as divorce, abortion, homosexuality, capital punishment. Reform here has been left by Government and to some extent by the Law Commission to the individual initiative of the private backbench Member of Parliament. Is this a satisfactory way of obtaining well thought out, well prepared legislation? Sir Leslie?

SCARMAN Well, first my respect for backbencher initiative in the House of Commons is unlimited. I think they have done marvellous work and amongst the heroes I would include A. P. Herbert in the thirties. I think that his tradition is still being nobly carried on by certain members of the House of Commons. Is it a satisfactory way of developing your law? Of course it is not. This is no fault of the private Member. He merely does not have the resources available to enable him to put before the House of Commons – I use Roscoe Pound's words – 'well-drawn comprehensive legislation'. But until we have the sort of system that Lord Devlin and others round this table have been describing let us have the backbencher rather than nothing at all.

ZANDER Lord Devlin, you have put forward a suggestion that the Law Commission itself might have a certain limited, delegated legislative power to do minor adjustment and minor clearing-up of anomalies.[1] How do you think this would in fact work?

DEVLIN Well, I have never asked Sir Leslie what he thinks of that, but it seems to me that somebody ought to have it. My experience as a judge has been that very often you have a regulation or an Act of Parliament, and it is just incomplete. Some point has been totally overlooked. You have to stretch and torture the words and put them on to a rack in order to get at what

[1] *Law Society's Gazette*, 1966, pp. 460-1.

your decision should be. Now much the best sort of solution to that type of case is, I think, frankly to admit that it is something that has not been thought of, that the law needs a little addition let into it or it needs a patch put on it. And one way of doing this is to say to the judge, 'Well, you ought to do it at the time.' That raises large problems. Another way of doing it is to say, when the case is over and when the judge has said, as he frequently does, 'this is a case where I am afraid I am compelled to do injustice to one side or the other because it has not been thought of by the legislature,' that that case goes straight to the Law Commission. And if it goes straight to the Law Commission, I would like to see the Law Commission with power to put the patch on. Parliament can take it off whenever it wants to. (Mind you, the Law Commission has a lot of other things to do, it would have to have a department to deal with it and be much larger than it is). It would be recognised that it is simply a temporary way of making the law work until the subject next comes before the House. If it is one of these regular subjects like rent restrictions or companies or something that is reviewed periodically, it will come before the House within a matter of a few years or so and until it does, let the Law Commission have a subordinate legislative power. Now would that work, Sir Leslie, do you think?

SCARMAN I do not think it would, Lord Devlin. I really don't. It would also be contrary to the views to which I subscribe. I am extremely anxious that the Law Commission should in fact design the future development of the law, and I am extremely anxious that it should deal rapidly with defects of the law exposed by the courts. Those are really the two functions of the Law Commission. The immediate remedial response and at the same time the long-term planning of the law's development. But even in the field of immediate remedial response I believe that the people, through their representative institutions, should have the right to say 'Aye or No: is the law going to be changed?' And let me just give you one word of caution from my experience in the Law Commission. When we began there we included in our first programme a number of miscellaneous items which we believed were only of limited importance, had been looked at before, and could rapidly lead to a number of limited law-reform proposals. Almost without exception every one of them proved to raise far greater issues than appeared on first sight. It would be quite wrong to have dealt with those on a quick patch system. Had we done so we would have torn the calico elsewhere. On the whole I am here cautious and for once unambitious.

LESTER I must say that I agree with Sir Leslie and not with Lord Devlin. It seems to me that apart from the constitutional problem of referring matters of that kind to the Law Commission for patching, there are other disadvantages. In the United States Professor Bickel, the Constitutional Law expert, has described the American Bench as the least dangerous branch of government; in this country it would be described more accurately as the least active branch of government. Traditionally it is the branch of government which abstains from making laws and deciding what the law ought to be. Now with an ever-growing body of statute law it is vital that judges should not be in the frame of mind where they feel able easily to refer gaps in the legislation to another body, whether it is Parliament or the Law Commission. On the contrary, I would urge that the rules of statutory interpretation as they now exist ought to be reformed to make it clearer that the judge's function is to presume rationality on the part of Parliament and to try to give effect to a rational intent even where there appear to be gaps in the literal language of the statute. There are of course jurisprudential difficulties about giving judges a more active role, but I would be very reluctant to encourage them to see their job as being what I think another American once described as penny-in-the-slot, automatic jurisprudence.

DEVLIN I see a difficulty about that. I follow entirely the objection to the Law Commission doing it, based largely on the grounds that nobody other than Parliament must make law. But to say 'don't let the Law Commission do it, let the judges do it themselves' seems to me to be encountering much greater difficulty and in a much greater form. You then have the judges making law instead of Parliament and the judges are inevitably much less well equipped, because while the Law Commission can get in other people and find out what the social answer is as well as the legal answer, the judge could only produce a sort of legal answer to it.

LESTER But the judges do make law at present, in many ways; often by deciding to abstain, they are making law; the decision not to do something can amount to a decision to do something in practice. If one takes cases involving the criminal law, the Shaw case – the Ladies Directory case[1] – in which the courts developed the crime of conspiracy to corrupt public morals, was a classic example of the making of law by judges, and what I would say is that whether or not one agrees with the Shaw decision there are inevitably going to be enormous delays in legislative reform by an overworked Parliament.

DEVLIN But then why do you prefer the judges to the Law Commission?

LESTER Because I think that the Law Commission has a different function, which is a function of consolidation and codification rather than dealing with the gaps and interstices in Statute Law and because I think that a healthy judiciary is a judiciary which is concerned with the implications of its decision. If you deprive the judiciary of speculation about where its decisions will lead in a social context you lead to bad law.

DEVLIN No, I must disagree with that. I think that would be an unhealthy judiciary. My idea of a healthy judiciary is a judiciary that is not concerned with where the law leads to.

LESTER Can I give two examples of what I have in mind? In the field of Constitutional and Administrative Law, the English judiciary has a much less active role than the American judiciary, and most Commonwealth and continental courts. Now that seems to me to be an example where judicial activism, if I

[1] *Shaw v. Director of Public Prosecutions* [1962] A.C. 220.

can use that phrase, would provide remedies for the individual, where at present they do not exist. And it seems to me that, whether one is concerned with matters involving central or local government, the English bench could be more active than it is. The second field in which I should have thought that one could have a more active judiciary would be in the field of contract law. Exemption clauses, standard contracts, and so on, are classic cases where we have built up a system of law on the principle of *laissez-faire*, where the judiciary tends to be reluctant to intervene (though it has increasingly done so in the last decade), and when more judicial intervention would be desirable.

DEVLIN Well I am afraid my ideas of health and activity in the judiciary are very different from yours.

ZANDER Sir Leslie, you see the private Member of Parliament playing a role in law reform. Do you see the judge playing an equally important or a more important role?

SCARMAN I see the judge playing a role in the development of the law but not in law reform. Listening to the debate that has arisen between Anthony Lester and Lord Devlin, I find myself agreeing with parts of each and disagreeing profoundly with parts of each, and I believe that they were each approaching the topic from different backgrounds. Let me explain what I mean. If you had a completely codified law, then I think there would be an important role for the judge, in applying the principle to be found stated in those codes and in interpreting the law. If the law were completely codified and the code was kept under review by a body like the Law Commission, I would have no objection to the judge being more activist, that is to say, looking to the principle and applying it, even in cases where he could find no direct application in the statute. But when one comes to the judge making law, as I agree the judges did make law in Shaw's case, then I am wholly with Lord Devlin. I do not believe the judge is equipped, or ought to be equipped, to make law. When a judge is dealing with a case, he has only such evidence as is given in court and he has his knowledge of the law. He has no other information available at all. When one is reforming the law, as one say has to do in the Law Commission, one has, as Lord Devlin has said, the whole array of social enquiry at one's disposal and it is one's job to use it. In fact you can only reform the law by straying far away from those issues upon which relevant evidence alone can be given in court. The court is not the proper place to manufacture new law.

DEVLIN I do not want to form a quick and unholy alliance with Sir Leslie in order to overwhelm Mr Lester, but really I do not disagree with anything that you have just said, Sir Leslie. That is to say that the distinction is between law reform and the active application of the principle in the law. That I would accept, but any sort of law reforming, no.

LESTER Well, I am overwhelmed by the alliance, but all I would like to add is this, that firstly I did disapprove of the Shaw case as an example of judicial activism. But where I think the judges do make law, though one does not always realise it, is in interpreting statutes. Very often a limited, narrow interpretation of, shall we say, a social security statute or industrial relations statute is tantamount to making law. It then takes Parliament ten or fifteen years to unmake the law. What I would prefer to see is statutory interpretation more closely in touch with the rational legislative intent, and what I am trying to say is that better statutory interpretation would lead to less need for periodic bouts of statutory amendment.

DEVLIN Get your statute well drawn and comprehensively drawn and then the judges will really have power to develop the law within their own limitations, but until your statute law is well drawn and comprehensively drawn, I myself fear judicial intervention in the process of law reform.

LESTER I think I agree with that.

ZANDER But Sir Leslie, one of the features of the brave new world under the Law Commission, with codes well and comprehensively drafted, is also the general principle which you have yourself alluded to. Now when one has general principles, this will throw on to the judges a much greater responsibility to develop the law in what Parliament and the Law Commission conceive to be socially useful ways. Is this a role which the judges are really equipped to perform?

SCARMAN I believe they are, and I hope that there will be Law Commission proposals for improving the aids to judicial interpretation of statutes. If one can make available to the judges as much information as possible as to the intent of Parliament in passing statutes, and if one can see to the drafting of the statutes, that they are, in the phrase I have already used, well drawn and comprehensive, then I would welcome judicial development of the law relying upon the code as giving the judge the principle of the matter.

ZANDER Lord Devlin, you once said that the judges of England have rarely been original thinkers or great jurists, they have been craftsmen rather than creators, they have needed the stuff of morals to be supplied to them, so that out of it they could fashion law; when they have had to make their own stuff, their work is inferior. If they are supplied with a broad general statement from the Law Commission enacted by Parliament, how will they be able to grapple with this in terms of seeing behind it the social purpose and then dealing with it in the way that the Law Commission and Parliament intended.

DEVLIN Well, I think it would not be the traditional way in which the English judicial mind at present works. I think that it is reluctant to exercise discretion. You frequently find when the statute gives a judge a discretion there is a tendency, particularly in the Chancery Division, to exercise it as sparingly as possible, or not at all. I think that it ought to be something a little more if possible than the broad statement of principle; start a new idea and the judges will make it work even if it means introducing quite novel conceptions. For example, the Rent Acts introduced the idea of the statutory tenant. In the Trading with the Enemy legislation they did not hesitate to make a business into a legal personality and treat it as if it were. Judges will do that, but I think that if you give them just a statement of principle, they will move too slowly really, they will move too cautiously, and of course they have to wait till it comes up, and the whole thing will take too long. But give them a bit more than that, give them a blue-print, and even though they might dislike it at first sight, they will see it is their job to make it work and they will make it work.

ZANDER Anthony Lester, you have supported the idea of judicial activism. Do you have confidence that the judiciary will be able to manage with this much broader discretion that might fall upon them in this new type of legislation?

LESTER I am apprehensive but I would be prepared to take the risk. As I see it, the role of legislation of the kind we have been talking about would be partly to declare public policy, to set out broad principles for the guidance of judges leaving them to apply the principles to particular cases. Now if I can take three fields that we have talked about this evening: Firstly, race relations law. That is a wholly new declaration of public policy and there Parliament, I think rightly, has decided that the judges ought to be guided in interpreting it by lay assessors and the County Court judges will be assisted in this way. That seems to me to be a sensible step as a way of helping the judges with these new concepts. Secondly, industrial relations legislation is likely to come forward in the next year and it seems what is contemplated is more law to be decided by the industrial tribunals again with lay assessors from both sides of industry, and there again I should have thought that was a good thing. The third field that we mentioned, administrative and constitutional law, which is perhaps the most important and most difficult, there I think I would be apprehensive of giving the ordinary judges of ordinary courts the very wide constitutional functions that one sees on the Continent and in America and I should have thought at the very least one needed a special administrative division of the High Court, perhaps assisted by retired senior civil servants, dealing with principles of fair administration and not leaving them at large. I think that in terms of our education as lawyers, and our background in practice as lawyers, we are not at the moment well equipped to interpret broad codes and these are all techniques which would make it more effective.

ZANDER Sir Leslie, would you agree?

SCARMAN I think our system of education could be improved in order to enable us to interpret law in its social context. The real change is to ensure that a lawyer is not merely a lawyer, or that he has experience in other disciplines and in other walks of life. In the old days, there was the awful vicious circle of the man who went to school and then went from school to university, then went from university to teaching and spent the rest of his life teaching. So a young man or a woman who just reads law at a university, then goes to the Inns of Court School of Law to become a barrister, then goes into barristers' Chambers and spends the rest of his life arguing questions in the County Court or in the High Court, is not equipped on that education to do the kind of job that needs to be done, if the legal system is to develop consistently. On the question of laymen in the law, I myself have never viewed with horror the bringing of lay assessors or expert assessors on to the judicial bench. This seems to me to be no more than a development of the old Common Law practice of involving the layman in the administration of justice. In the old days this was done by use of the jury and by use of the lay magistracy. It may be that the jury no longer has so important a function to play as it did have. But laymen still have an important function. The jury box did represent a vital element in the administration of the Common Law, the lay element; if the jury has to go I would like to see the lay element come in somewhere else, in a situation more consistent with the requirements of modern life. I wholly agree with the basic thinking of Anthony Lester on this point.

ZANDER Lord Devlin, coming to the end of this discussion, now that you have retired from judicial office, looking back and looking forward, would you say that the prospect of the next fifty years is in any way different as a result of the advent of the Law Commission from the last fifty years?

DEVLIN Well, fifty years is so short a time in the life of the law, I hesitate to say that the prospect would be very different in the next than it was in the past. The idea of the Law Commission has made a profound difference, but how much is it going to be backed up? That is the question that one will have to wait and get the answer to before I would want to make a prophecy. And in particular how much is its work going to be used, because it is no use having a Law Commission that is turning out this stuff if it is faced with what is virtually a blank wall with no means of taking it any further. It will not be until I see the government of the day devising some effective means of using the Law Commission's work that I should start making prophecies about the next fifty years.

SCARMAN I agree with everything that Lord Devlin has just said. I would make only one comment and it is this. I see the Law Commission as a legal institution that will work its good, if it is going to work any good, slowly. I would not like to see the Law Commission measured against a short span of time. It is here to do its work over an indefinite period of time.

TOMORROW'S LAWYERS

An inquiry into the education of lawyers compiled by WILLIAM PLOWDEN

with PROFESSOR J. N. D. ANDERSON
PROFESSOR R. S. BROWN
PATRICK LEFEVRE
CHARLES MORRISON
HOWARD OWENS
PROFESSOR T. B. SMITH
PROFESSOR W. TWINING
J. F. WARREN
BEN WHITAKER, M.P.
MICHAEL ZANDER
A practising barrister

PLOWDEN I will begin with a quotation from the report of the Select Committee on Legal Education of 1846.

> The present state of legal education, both professional and unprofessional, is extremely unsatisfactory and incomplete and in striking contrast and inferiority to such education in all the more civilised states of Europe and America. The student is left to his own individual exertions and no legal education worthy of the name of a public nature is to be found.

120 years later this statement, perhaps slightly qualified and elaborated, would still be widely echoed. Patrick Lefevre, a Bar student, describes the training of today's intending barristers.

LEFEVRE It is very difficult to describe the education of a barrister because basically there is no form of compulsory education, no institutional training which a barrister must do to qualify. The only thing he must do is to take his exams. The schools of law at universities do provide some education and the professions themselves also provide some facilities. They are optional facilities. The lectures are not mandatory and the entry system to those professional schools is a liberal one, that is to say the conditions of entry are minimal. You only need to have two 'A' Levels. There is no control of the entry into the school. The result is that we have a very big student population of several thousands and very poor facilities. We have lectures with several hundred students which are occasionally completely overflowing. We have tutorials the size of most English university lectures – that is presuming you can even get into the tutorial. In other words the facilities are totally inadequate. The effect of this exam system and of the very over-crowded facilities (the exam system meaning that one has to cram for exams rather than be educated) is a very heavy failure rate. An average university failure rate is under ten per cent, whereas our failure rate is something like seventy per cent. The former French Minister of Education described the French exam system, which is very much akin to ours, as something like organising a shipwreck to pick out the best swimmers. With a failure rate of seventy per cent including people retaking the exam we are very much in that position.

PLOWDEN It would be untrue to say that nothing has changed in the education of lawyers in the past 120 years. But the present scene would still be recognisable to the Select Committee. Things are still wrong.

This should matter to us. Any society should take an interest in the quality of its lawyers. In Britain, as in many other societies where relationships and activities are regulated by formal laws, it is the task of professional lawyers to make authoritative decisions on how those laws apply in particular cases. This gives them great influence. It is being increasingly loudly and persuasively argued that English lawyers are not properly qualified for this responsibility. One of the major reasons for this is said to be the way in which they are trained for the job.

But today, after a century of near-stagnation, the training of lawyers is being actively discussed. And the emphasis in this discussion is very much on change. The lawyers themselves have been talking about change. Several major questions need to be answered:

Why is change necessary?

Why has the need for change now been accepted by lawyers?

What are the changes proposed?

What will be their effects?

Will they satisfy all the demands for reform?

And lurking beneath all these questions is another which is much more basic: what are lawyers for? What is the role in modern society for which they must be prepared?

First, to establish the basic facts about the structure and training of the profession. The structure is relatively simple. There are three main groups of English lawyers: about 22,000 practising solicitors, just over 2,000 qualified barristers, and around 250 full-time members of the judiciary, whose higher appointments are made from the ranks of the successful barristers. There are also several thousand qualified barristers and solicitors working as salaried employees in central and local government, industry and commerce.

The details of the education of lawyers are indescribably complex. But a few simple principles underlie all. First, a university degree in law, or in anything else, is neither necessary nor at the same time sufficient for entry to the profession. It is possible to qualify simply by passing the professional examinations and by serving a term of apprenticeship: the law graduate is exempted from the first part of the professional examination, but even he must take the second part. In fact nearly all barristers entering practice today have some sort of degree, and most have law degrees. Only about half today's practising solicitors have a degree; the same is true of the present generation of trainee solicitors, so this proportion is unlikely to change for some time.

Both the Bar and the solicitors provide a certain amount of teaching for their examinations. But only those intending solicitors who have no law degree need attend the solicitors' College of Law, and – as Patrick Lefevre said – no intending barrister need go to the courses provided by the Bar's Council of Legal Education. Most barristers, and many solicitors, prepare for their professional examinations at a 'crammer's'.

Both barristers and solicitors must also spend a period as an apprentice to a practising lawyer; the barrister must spend at least one year as a 'pupil' in Chambers, the solicitor at least two years as an 'articled clerk'.

Teaching, examining and qualification are quite separate for each side of the profession; qualifying for one side gives no automatic entrée to the other.

Finally, judges: no special educational qualifications are required to become a judge.

These requirements may sound reasonably thorough. But it might be of interest to note how they do these things elsewhere. In the United States, for instance. Professor Ralph S. Brown of the Yale University Law School describes the minimum requirement for the American lawyer.

BROWN Practically no one in the United States begins his law studies until he has finished university. Indeed in most states it is no longer possible to be admitted to practice unless one has sat a full law course, preceded by a regular undergraduate course. Furthermore with us the undergraduate course is four years as against three years here and then after that you have three years of law school so it is a total of seven years of schooling after secondary school.

PLOWDEN But for comparison there is no need to go as far as the United States. Over the border in Scotland the traditional training for the law is a law degree, especially for 'advocates', that is to say, barristers. The regulations have been changed recently, but both sides of the profession now accept a three-year LL.B. as sufficient academic qualification for entry, provided that certain prescribed subjects have been taken. Both sides then require a period of apprenticeship; advocates must do not only nine months' pupillage, but also twenty-one months in a solicitor's office.

These two comparisons at least show that there are other

ways of training lawyers. The argument that the English way is inadequate takes two quite different forms: first, that they are poorly prepared for the job; secondly, that the nature of the job itself is misconceived.

Criticism of the preparation for the job centres both on the examinations, and on the teaching – or lack of teaching – for them, and on the apprenticeship stage. For both sides of the profession, the original aim of the examinations was to find out whether the candidate had a full knowledge of the existing law. Today, this is an impossible objective; the enormous growth in statute legislation in particular means that there is simply too much law. The profession largely accepts this. Mr John Warren is Secretary of the Law Society's Education and Training Committee:

WARREN In the not so very distant past there were in fact four papers in the solicitor's final examination, the range of which could cover the whole of English law. New branches of the law are expanding fast, in fields such as tax, companies, industrial relations, air and space travel. We have now realised that trying to teach a little about everything is quite impossible. The wide range of the syllabus means that the examination becomes very largely a memory test, there is so much to learn. For our present Part II the student is faced with some 4,000 pages of textbooks and it is almost literally true to say that he can expect to be asked a question on any one of those 4,000 pages. It is, I think, impossible to teach properly for an examination with so wide a scope as that, and almost impossible also to learn for it. It is just a question of the teachers forcing stuff into the minds of the candidates, and the candidates trying to remember as much as they can.

PLOWDEN Even so, areas of modern law such as rent legislation, hire purchase, factory accidents, national insurance are barely covered, if at all, in the professional examinations. And there are similar gaps in many university curricula. What's more, many critics suggest that there are new subjects of which a modern lawyer should know something. Ben Whitaker, M.P., himself a qualified barrister, suggests a couple.

WHITAKER First of all a basic grasp of criminology and penology, because I think it is somewhat absurd that lawyers from a totally different field are expected to award sentences without probably ever having in their lives visited a prison or a borstal or an approved school to which they are going to commit people perhaps for many years. And secondly I think it would be extremely useful for lawyers if there was a basic grasp of medical and psychiatric terminology at least. So that when they meet medical expert witnesses in court, which frequently happens in all kinds of cases, both accident cases and criminal cases, at least the lawyers and the doctors will then speak the same language. One gets distressing cases at present where they seem to be talking two totally different foreign languages.

PLOWDEN Some practising lawyers still argue for the traditional approach, claiming that to have covered the ground, however superficially, at least gives one an idea of the outline of the subject and of the main problems. It is because the outline itself is changing so fast, that this is no longer a useful approach.

But to discuss the content of the exams may be to put the cart before the horse. As already indicated, at the Bar in particular there has for long been serious dissatisfaction with the teaching. Until very recently, the Council of Legal Education had no full-time teaching staff. The over-crowding which makes the teaching provided more inadequate even than it might be stems from a problem peculiar to the Bar. The overwhelming majority of Bar students – up to three-quarters at its peak in recent years – are from Commonwealth countries, mainly Africa and India. Charles Morrison, Dean of the Council of Legal Education, explains why the Bar feels it necessary to look after these students.

MORRISON We have a peculiar duty here. One of the significant things in legal history is the spread of English law throughout many Commonwealth countries – as significant in legal history as the spread of Roman law. So that we have English judiciaries, English legal systems, English law, all over the world, and we therefore have a duty to train barristers for practice in an English-type system. This, therefore, means that we have to go on training, at least for the foreseeable future, a large number of barristers from overseas. At least until the law schools in their own countries are able to cope with the numbers involved.

PLOWDEN But unfortunately, however good the Bar's intentions, the results benefit neither the few English lawyers who try to rely on the facilities of the Council of Legal Education, nor the Commonwealth students themselves. Michael Zander, Lecturer in Law at the London School of Economics, suggests that everybody loses under the present system.

ZANDER They do hold back the education of English lawyers in the sense that standards are rather lower than they might otherwise be because of the need to allow at least a reasonable proportion of the overseas students to pass. I think the fault here is in allowing students to enter on the training who really have relatively little prospect of success. The Bar Council and the Council of Legal Education are trying to do something about this. I do not, myself, think that it is terribly useful for an overseas student to come to this country to learn his law, particularly under the existing conditions. I would think that the overseas student would be much better served by studying locally and this, of course, is the trend. But even in countries where local law schools are now developing, a good number of students still think it is worth their while to come, not I fear because of the marvellous education which they get here, but more for social reasons of prestige. They can go back and call themselves Barrister-at-Law at the English Bar and know that this has a certain *cachet* which would not be available if they trained locally.

PLOWDEN In any case, it is not at all certain that developing states need more English barristers-at-law, as opposed to engineers, doctors or architects (and the less so since their professions are 'fused', i.e. do not have the rigid barrister/solicitor distinction). But the Council of Legal Education, whose attitude to the problem seems in the past to have rested mainly on the hope that it would soon disappear of its own accord, has demanded higher educational requirements of all students admitted from April 1969. This may well reduce the numbers of Commonwealth students qualified for admission.

As important as the professional examinations, and now probably more unsatisfactory, is the apprenticeship requirement. At its best, the method of learning by watching can be quite effective, if unsystematic. A practising barrister describes the value to him of his own time as a pupil.

BARRISTER Certainly so far as I was concerned as a pupil, my pupillage was invaluable to me. The pupil sits in the same room as his pupil master. He does dummy runs on all the sets of papers that come into his master. He is there at all conferences, and his master, in order to clear his mind on the point on which he will shortly have to advise – whether to call this witness, whether to put the case this way or that way – relies to a great extent on his pupil, if only as a sounding board and someone to argue with. You learn much more about the practice of law from seeing at very close quarters someone doing it than you ever would either from books or from practical training schemes.

PLOWDEN But at its worst, the system is disastrous. As a whole, it is erratic. At the Bar the most successful Chambers – and those whose methods might be thought the most worth studying – are by definition the busiest, and their members are thus the least able to find time to explain to their pupils what is going on. It can be extremely hard to find a place in Chambers, especially for women and foreign students; the system is private and unco-ordinated, and still rests at least partly on chance and on connections. Its latent inadequacies have been greatly intensified in recent years. Charles Morrison explains:

MORRISON In the course of the last few years it has become apparent that better teaching arrangements can be, and should be, arrived at. In recent years work at the Bar has become much more plentiful for young members which means that the young barrister now goes into court on his own much earlier than he would have done in earlier times. In the past he was able, after pupillage, to spend some time in Chambers learning his job and becoming expert in his own field. Now he goes into court quite soon after being called, so that he needs to be much more fully trained at the moment of call than he has been hitherto.

PLOWDEN The only advantage of this situation is that, by sparing the young barrister a wait of possibly some years for his first brief and his first fee, it lessens his need for private means of support. But it is not likely to produce a very high standard of advocacy. Service under articles is equally unsatisfactory. Howard Owens, an articled clerk and secretary of a group representing the articled clerks, spoke for them at large.

OWENS There are two things primarily wrong. The first thing is that of the lack of sufficient payment. The average payment for articled clerks is at the moment about £6 15s. a week. The second thing is the general system itself. Articles, as they stand at present, simply are not working because of the conditions in the office. Some people in the office are simply glorified office boys. Others are not getting the sort of training they deserve from their principals, because the old idea of the principal/pupil relationship has broken down. So that principals – that is to say, practising solicitors – generally speaking no longer have the time or possibly make the time to give their articled clerks individual tuition. Some sort of course or some sort of training is necessary to supplement people's experience in the office.

PLOWDEN On the financial side, Mr Owens gave the average wage. He might have added that in some areas the weekly wage of an articled clerk is as low as £3 10s.; and that there are still today a few articled clerks who have paid their firms a premium for the privilege of joining them. The prospect for a trainee without some other means of support is thus fairly depressing – and especially for the non-graduate, whose period of articles is five years.

All the criticisms heard so far are made equally by qualified members of the profession. In a recent survey,[1] no less than eighty-three per cent of barristers of under five years' standing thought current training arrangements inadequate; sixty-eight per cent of young solicitors agreed with them. (Each side of the profession tends to think its own task the more demanding: the barrister will point out that he must be able to give a convincing solo performance in court, while the solicitor always has law books, telephone and partners to hand; the solicitor will reply that he must give his advice off-the-cuff to a client demanding an answer, while the barrister never appears unless briefed by a solicitor.) These criticisms of apprenticeship are now accepted by the leaders of the profession. John Warren explains how the Law Society views the whole notion of the articled clerk.

WARREN Instead of the articled clerk being what you might call the officer cadet in the office, who was there as a learner but with somewhat special status, he has now become in fact an employee who is hoping to learn at the same time. That has brought about a considerable change in the whole concept of service under articles and has had two results. One is that the training of the articled clerk has, by and large, deteriorated. There have always been complaints from articled clerks that they have not been properly trained under articles, but I think that the volume and validity of those complaints has increased in recent years. Secondly, the problem which is now present in a great many, though not all, parts of the country is that even good calibre potential recruits are being lost to the profession because they cannot find a solicitor ready to accept them under articles. An articled clerk is a time-consuming person if he

[1]Wilson, 'A Survey of Legal Education in the U.K.', Vol. IX, *Journal of the Society of Public Teachers of Law*, June 1966, pp. 73 and 83.

is going to be taught. He takes up office space, which is at a premium. And apart from any salary which is paid by the principal from his own pocket, the principal also has to pay National Health Insurance contributions and S.E.T.

PLOWDEN Solicitors have also for a long time complained about the difficulty of transferring from one side of the profession to the other, especially since, in their view, their examinations are much harder than the barristers'. One effect of this has been to limit the chances of former solicitors getting on to the Bench. It is also arguable, though unprovable, that the effective need to make so early a final choice between one side or the other deters able recruits from joining either.

Independent critics and the profession are thus broadly agreed that today's lawyers are inadequately prepared even for their existing tasks. Many critics take the argument a long way beyond this. They suggest that it is less the training of lawyers that needs changing than the whole conception of their role in society, and that from this must follow even more far-reaching changes in the way they are prepared for this role. There seem to be two parts to this argument. The first runs that the development of a welfare society creates a complex of new relationships which need regulating by law; groups in society are given new claims on other groups and on the community at large. They need the help of lawyers in asserting these claims. For lawyers, this implies new skills, and perhaps also new attitudes. Michael Zander puts this case.

ZANDER One wants lawyers who are technically competent not only in the fields in which they now work but also in fields in which in the future they either might want to work or have to work. And at the same time one wants lawyers who understand the society in which they live, who are energetic, who show ingenuity in using the particular intellectual tools of their trade in ways which are socially beneficial, not only to the fairly limited range of clients whom they now serve but also to the much wider concept of the community at large that one hopes will be included in legal services for the community in the future. One wants lawyers to get into all sorts of situations to help consumers, to help tenants, to help old-age pensioners, to help all kinds of individuals who at the present time have legal problems and do not get professional advice when they often need it.

PLOWDEN The second part of this argument sees law as a creative social instrument which does not merely regulate but helps actually to shape relationships, to define claims on society. This means that lawyers need some articulate ideas about society, and about the place of law in it. The present Lord Chancellor wrote some years ago that in a welfare state lawyers

> should be aware of the function of law in society and appreciate the interaction between law and social and economic progress.

Michael Zander suggests one way in which lawyers could bring such an awareness to bear.

ZANDER One would like the lawyers themselves to exercise more ingenuity and initiative than they now do in looking for situations. The whole legal system should respond more to the idea of social change through the courts – through the test case as a means of effecting social change in addition, of course, to the much more comprehensive means of changing society through legislation.

PLOWDEN So far the discussion has centred on barristers and solicitors. But there is another group of lawyers to whom everything that has been said about the training of barristers might be supposed to apply with even greater force: the higher judiciary. Their key position might be thought to call for special training. What is more, they labour under peculiar difficulties, as Ben Whitaker explains.

WHITAKER The danger, I think, is that the successful lawyer becomes isolated because of the amount of work he is doing.

He is so busy in court and having conferences with his clients that he does not have a chance to do any background research or work, and it is these successful lawyers who tend to be made judges. So the result is that the High Court judge tends to come from a very lonely and successful sector of society, and has not had much chance to mix outside the legal profession. The trouble is that a man who has been a brilliant and experienced lawyer at, say, tax or divorce is appointed to be a High Court judge and is then thrown in at the deep end and is expected to be a specialist in criminal work. He may not have done a criminal case for the last twenty years.

PLOWDEN None of the proposals which have been mentioned so far, whether for training lawyers better or for producing a different sort of lawyer, are very new in themselves. But in the last couple of years all have been given an unprecedented force and currency as a result of the setting-up by the Lord Chancellor of a committee to consider the future of legal education in England and Wales. It is chaired by Mr Justice Ormrod, who himself has also qualified, and has practised and taught, as a doctor of medicine. Its members include representatives of all the main interested parties – solicitors, barristers, teachers – and one non-lawyer, the Regius Professor of Medicine at Oxford University.

The establishment of this committee, and the legal profession's new willingness to accept the need for change, can be attributed to a legitimate mixture of self-interest and self-criticism on the part of the profession. Self-interest, in that the profession's favoured position and valuable monopolies – including especially the monopoly of regulating its own affairs – will prove increasingly hard to defend against outside critics unless it can appear slightly more forward-looking, flexible and socially aware than it has done in the past. The solicitors' demands for an end to the rigid barriers between the two sides of the profession add weight here; their constant pressure for ease of transfer is seen by some at the Bar as one of the main reasons for present developments. The solicitors think this overstated; they slightly deprecate what they see as the Bar Council's morbid fears of a takeover by the Law Society, and suggest that there are more important reasons for reform, such as the need to end the present wasteful duplication of training arrangements.

Self-interest is present also in that lawyers are in danger of losing business, as they have already lost much work in the taxation field to the accountants and the banks. Ben Whitaker makes the point.

WHITAKER I think there is a considerable amount of evidence, and lawyers themselves are coming to realise this, that the present traditional law courts in Britain, partly due to the training of lawyers, are losing touch with the mainstream of litigation in society today. I think there has lately been a remarkable growth of quasi-legal courts outside our traditional framework – for example, there is the Immigration Appeals Court being set up; there are all the tribunals which are used more and more and hardly ever get in the public eye; there is the Race Conciliation machinery and the proposed new Commission on Industrial Relations. All these are examples of a quasi-legal framework being set up in different sectors of our society because the normal legal machinery is felt to be too slow, or not specialised enough. And lawyers themselves obviously have come to lose as a result of this and that I think is one of the reasons why lawyers are taking a long, hard look at their present approach to society.

PLOWDEN But there is also self-criticism. There is much genuine dissatisfaction within the profession both with the training for the job and, to a lesser extent, with the conception of the job itself. There have already been changes – for instance, the appointment of Mr Morrison as the first full-time Dean of the Council of Legal Education, and the raising of educational standards for Bar students.

Everyone with an interest in the education of lawyers is now putting forward views to the Ormrod Committee. Both the Bar and the solicitors have proposed changes which go far beyond anything publicly suggested by the profession in the past. Broadly, both have proposed that the normal educational qualification for the intending lawyer should be a law degree, and that the profession should supplement this with a period of intensive and systematic practical training. The old dominance of the professional examinations, and the cramming which goes with them, is to end; apprenticeship, though not abolished, is to become less important. For the first time a distinction is clearly made between education – left to the universities – and training – left to the profession. The basic education is to be the same for both sides of the profession; the solicitors have gone further in proposing that much even of the training should also be common. In March 1969 the Council of Legal Education announced that the new arrangements at the Bar would apply to all students admitted after the end of that month.

The major innovation in all this is the emphasis given to the law degree. The many critics who have scoffed at the idea of a so-called 'learned' profession which does not demand more than 'A' Levels should approve. If the modern lawyer cannot hope to master all the details of the law, at least he can be familiar with the principles which underlie it. But if a law degree is to have this new status, can it continue to be the same kind of law degree? Michael Zander sees room for improving the quality of the university teaching of law.

ZANDER I think the university legal education at the moment is not terribly good; not nearly as good as it should be. It is not sufficiently orientated towards contemporary problems and it is not sufficiently liberal – it tends to be superficial, based mainly on learning of rules which is the very antithesis of education in the proper sense. The universities have to abandon the idea that you can teach law by studying a textbook from start to finish. First of all we need new textbooks which explore legal problems from a much wider variety of points of view than simply a recitation of the rules. We need to bring into our law courses the economics, the sociology, the psychology, the criminology, all the extra-legal considerations which cannot adequately be tacked on by other courses. It is no good having a course in economics for law students. What you need to do is to bring in the economics into the Property course or into the Contract course and this is very difficult because the law teachers are not economists, whilst the economists do not have the interests of law students sufficiently in mind really to know how to do it. Probably what you need is something that is now happening in America more than here – namely joint courses – courses run by lawyers and economists, lawyers and psychiatrists, lawyers and members of other disciplines, to try and zero in on the problems from these different points of view.

PLOWDEN These details apart, John Warren sees a problem of principle.

WARREN What sort of end-product is the law graduate to be? If a law degree is to be regarded as part of a gentleman's education, as for a very long time it was and perhaps still is at Oxbridge, that is one thing. If, on the other hand, the universities are going to be technical schools and aim at training deliberately for the professions, that is another thing. And that is why I take the view that one of the first points that the Ormrod Committee have to decide is where the universities fit into the general pattern of professional education, because until you have that settled you can't go on with a consideration of professional education.

PLOWDEN Perhaps it will no longer be possible to treat law as a subject for liberal education. Is it desirable to do so? Professor William Twining of Queen's University, Belfast, has no doubts.

TWINING I think that law is potentially a very rich, a very rewarding discipline in its own right. I think it has certain advantages over other social sciences. It provides an avenue into understanding society as potentially illuminating as any other social science. And yet continually one is forced to wrestle with very concrete, very specific, very intellectually demanding problems. I have no doubt at all that law should continue to be an intellectual discipline in its own right.

PLOWDEN The basic argument here is about the content of a law degree – and who should decide it. The Bar tends to argue that there must be some common basis of knowledge among the students coming to it for the practical training stage. If there is not, valuable time and resources may have to be spent on teaching students what they should know already. Though it may be noted that graduates of American law schools go out and practise in no less than fifty different states, and the District of Columbia, with slightly different legal systems.

But it looks certain that the teachers of law will insist on keeping alive the broader conception of a law degree, whatever the profession's demands. Half the university students reading law – and providing employment for law teachers – do not intend to practise as lawyers. It thus follows that such students will not be attracted by courses reshaped to meet the specific requirements of the profession. Professor J. N. D. Anderson, Director of the Institute of Advanced Legal Studies and President of the Society of Public Teachers of Law, explains how many teachers see the problem.

ANDERSON We think that it is exceedingly important that we should so devise our syllabus and our way of teaching that law as taught in the universities represents a liberal education and not merely a preparation for the practice of the law as a vocation. That is one thing. Then again the universities, as always, are exceedingly anxious to keep their independence. We do not want to have the practising profession dictating to us what we should teach or how we should teach it. In fact a number of universities are going a considerable way in experimentation in their law degrees, with regard to the subjects that are taught, and the manner of teaching them: teaching law for instance as one of the social sciences with far more relation to other aspects of contemporary life than merely the professional legal approach. And then again in a number of universities today we have mixed degrees. Law and Economics, or whatever it may be. So one of the problems between the universities and the professions is the attitude they are going to take to the training which is being given in the universities.

PLOWDEN How does it work elsewhere? No English lawyer I asked could tell me anything about the Scottish system, so I asked Professor Thomas Smith, of the Department of Scots Law at Edinburgh, to describe how the Scottish system works in practice.

SMITH Basically the training for the legal profession in Scotland is through the universities. Therefore the future advocate and the future solicitor have sat on the same benches in the university as students and they have taken substantially the same university courses. We have not in Scotland as in England for practical purposes a separate examination system for the two different sides of the profession. Now since our law students are trained in very much the same way, provided that they have done the same requisite practical training they can move quite easily from one side of the profession – solicitor to advocate or indeed from advocate to solicitor – and at the present time quite a number of our distinguished judges or distinguished counsel started in their profession as lawyers or solicitors before they decided that their special gifts were in the very individual profession of advocacy.

I think that relations between the universities and both sides of the profession in Scotland have been good – certainly there is willingness on either side to co-operate – and we in the universities welcome suggestions from the profession. Perhaps I should make this point: that a fair number of us who teach law in Scotland have had a certain amount of practical experience and, though I am an advocate myself, I think it is an advantage that a good number of our law teachers have been solicitors. In short, our professional qualifications are not merely paper qualifications and we do retain our contacts with our practising professional brethren. We have no sense in the universities that we are being dictated to, as to what we should teach or how we should teach it by the practising profession. We teach a core of subjects, a central core of subjects, which the professions require, but if I were making a selection of those legal subjects necessary to train a lawyer in Scotland I would probably choose substantially the same subjects. Now of course in addition there are a fair number of selective subjects which students in Scottish law faculties can choose from, and the profession in both its branches allows a certain flexibility of choice for completing the academic qualifications of an entrant to the profession.

PLOWDEN Comparisons may not always be wholly relevant. The American law degree, for example, is, after all, a graduate degree. Some think we should move a little closer to the Americans by at least insisting on a four-year undergraduate degree; on the basis of Scottish experience, this was Professor Smith's view. Others think that law is not a suitable subject for undergraduate teaching at all. The practising barrister we heard earlier expressed his doubts.

BARRISTER In problem questions that they have in law examinations, you have a nice neat tidy statement of facts, and to those facts you are meant to apply the law. That doesn't happen at all in practice, because it is very seldom that two sides to a dispute are agreed as to what exactly the facts of that dispute are. In the early stages of a problem, it usually comes to you as a large bundle of correspondence between businessmen on each side, and your first job is to go through what is often a haystack of letters and documents and discover from that haystack what the relevant facts are. Your first job is to define the problem, and it is only after you have defined the problem that there is any question of applying the law to it. I do not think that law is a good academic subject. The law schools in the universities, in an attempt to make it so, tend to philosophise overmuch about it and to fit individual decisions into a grand overall scheme or philosophy when this was not something that the court had in mind at all. The court was trying to do justice in the case before it and to do justice without outrage to the system of law in which that decision was reached, and academics seem to me really to make too much of the more philosophical concept of law. Law is a practical subject, and in so far as knowledge of it is necessary in the way that I have indicated, that knowledge seems to me to come much better in a postgraduate course rather than an ordinary degree course where education is perhaps more important than the acquisition of knowledge.

PLOWDEN On the other hand (and assuming that the problems of finance could be overcome) how much education can aspiring lawyers be persuaded to take? Professor Brown suggests that there may be limits.

BROWN I would say that in the United States there is a growing unrest among the students, and one form that this unrest is taking is an unwillingness to continue three years of law study along the lines that it has traditionally been, and by traditionally I mean for the last thirty, or forty, or fifty years. The natives, in other words, are getting restless and ask why, when they have been twelve years to school, four years to college, they need three years of law school before they are prepared to go out and qualify for practice.

PLOWDEN There are other related questions. The division between academic subjects, suitable for university teaching, and purely practical topics which can safely be left to the profession, is not a simple one to make. Professor Brown suggested that this separation might be bad for both sides.

BROWN There is not such a clear distinction between practical topics and academic topics and it may be that some branches of the law do not receive the proper attention they should from the standpoint of possible reform and improvement and the study of their history when they are separated and made simply the subject of instruction in the Inns of Court or equivalent schools, for admission to the profession. To have a large-scale period outside an academic setting, in which one is simply preparing for practice, does perhaps lead to an unwarranted separation of what are considered the academic branches of the law from the practical branches, a separation which I do not think is good for either side.

PLOWDEN Professor Twining felt that the most decisive arguments for such a division were not being fully brought out.

TWINING If and when it comes about I hope very much that people will realise that it has been done largely on grounds of administrative convenience and political expediency, rather than on educational grounds. I think that a great strength of law as an intellectual discipline is just that it does combine theory and practice, that it does involve the continuous interaction between the concrete and the abstract, between the realities of everyday life and serious, difficult, challenging, intellectual problems. Any educational framework which threatens to bring about an unhealthy relationship between theory and practice is dangerous.

PLOWDEN There is a more basic question still. Even assuming that the minor differences can be resolved, will the proposed changes cure the ailments of the legal profession? The problem here is that the diagnoses vary. The profession is aiming at the more systematic production of more competent lawyers. The radical critics want a different kind of lawyer altogether. An eminent judge with whom I discussed this explicitly rejected the wider function: the task of the Council of Legal Education, he said, was to train and produce efficient barristers, to serve the public in the lower courts – not to turn out legal philosophers. Many reformers do not see these courses as alternatives, which is perhaps to say that they want the best of both worlds, but there is a real conflict of objectives here. I asked Charles

Morrison his view of the task of the Council of Legal Education.

MORRISON We certainly have to think in terms of getting competent barristers in the courts to deal with immediate problems. We are not aiming to teach for the end of the century. This is not our problem. I think if it is anyone's problem it is one for the universities. But nevertheless, in our teaching we do hope that we shall make our students aware of the more general issues without attempting to turn out a social engineer in those terms. I hope that our view is not a narrow one. We certainly want to produce competent lawyers, trained to meet the kind of problems that face them immediately on practice, and, of course, to train our future judges. But although we have an immediate problem of training we hope also – at least I hope also – that we shall not be narrow about this and that once we have satisfied ourselves about the immediate form of training we shall be able to introduce a number of other subjects, perhaps not subjects of examination but at least subjects of teaching and discussion, which will broaden the view of the barrister.

PLOWDEN The Law Society, too, gave no hint in its evidence to the Ormrod Committee that there was anything to say about the changing role of the solicitor in modern society. Mr Warren speculated that a revised vocational course might aim to include a much wider spread of subjects, with talks on related professions, the Stock Exchange, financial affairs and so on. This, he thought, should provide a much better equipped solicitor. I suggested to him that even this implied a rather narrow view: was there no case for training the solicitor to be more of a 'social engineer'?

WARREN I think time is the main objection. Ideally I suppose a solicitor should have training in sociology and economics; some people would say he should be able to speak at least one modern European language fluently; he should have a knowledge of social problems and so on, and he should also have a fairly detailed knowledge of the law. If you are going to produce the ideal solicitor who has all this background, you are not going to get anybody qualified until they are about forty-five. This just is not possible.

PLOWDEN There seems to me to be much in this answer. In any case, it is not at all obvious that most intending lawyers want to be trained as social engineers. I asked Howard Owens whether articled clerks would be interested in proposals for reform which envisaged a different kind of solicitor.

OWENS They are interested in getting better training in the office, and equally in being paid more, since some of them simply cannot exist on what they are getting. I would not think they see themselves as carrying out a different role. Rather they see the need to be more efficient, better trained, and more specialised in their particular fields.

PLOWDEN Whatever the philosophy behind current proposals from the profession, they do not seem to touch, at least in the short term, various individual problems. How, for instance, does one deal with the question of keeping up to date the knowledge of lawyers in fields which may be rapidly developing?

WHITAKER In any approach I think it is going to be necessary that there should be regular refresher courses because obviously what the lawyer learns when he passes his exams in his twenties is going to be obsolete and inadequate by the time he becomes a judge, some twenty or thirty years later. The disadvantage of the system of voluntary retraining is that some lawyers are enterprising and go back voluntarily to try to catch up as to new developments. But those who are most in need of retraining usually do not go in for this.

PLOWDEN This last point ties in with one which seems to me crucial to any attempt to improve the service offered by lawyers to the community by improving their education. It is one thing to encourage lawyers to become better at their jobs: crude market forces alone will, in the end, dictate this. But what hopes are there that lawyers will feel any comparable pressures to do a better job in the wider sense envisaged by the radical reformers? The barrister, for instance, may reasonably grasp at the chance to acquire new knowledge and techniques that will help him to defend his client better. But why should he try to arouse the Bench's social conscience if he knows he can more effectively play on its prejudices? I choose this example advisedly; judges, who determine how the law applies to a case, determine also what kind of considerations are relevant to their decision. Michael Zander feels that the judges could often take a broader view than they do.

ZANDER The judge in the present system tends to view the arguments which can properly be brought to bear on a legal problem in a rather narrow framework. He sees extra-legal argument, argument for example on the economic or social consequences of particular rules, as being very peripheral. The extra-legal considerations should be brought more openly into the decision-making process of judges. The question, What ought the law to be? should be seen as a legitimate part of the question, What is the law? It is in fact implicit and yet at present it is excluded by the judges.

PLOWDEN A High Court judge with whom I discussed this point said that it would indeed be a great step forward when judges insisted, as he put it for example, on 'a decent plea in mitigation, and don't just accept a footling account of how much the client loves his family and so on . . .'

If there is anything in this point about the influence of the judges – and some lawyers will think I have overstated it – it would suggest that to see the full benefits of any improvements in the education of lawyers, we may need to wait at least until today's Bar students – or articled clerks – have themselves reached the Bench. But it will take even more than changes in individual lawyers to produce a different sort of profession. I asked Professor Anderson how far, in his view, the changes proposed in their education would produce a new kind of lawyer. He considered that lawyers educated in the traditional way – that is, without taking a law degree – were not equipped to ask the right questions.

ANDERSON They never had the opportunity to look at the law as a whole; to consider the law from the point of view of 'this is the law at the moment, but ought it to be the law in the future? Does it need to be reformed? Ought something to be done about it?' Now this is the sort of thing that we try to include in a law degree at the university – an approach which is in part new, jurisprudential and critical. And so inevitably, I think, different methods of training will produce, to some extent, a different type of lawyer. But, in the final resort, it will depend a great deal on the structure of the professions in the future, on the law reforms which the Law Commissioners are trying to bring in now, and indeed on reforms in regard not merely to the substance of the law, but the courts and their practice.

PLOWDEN It will also depend not only on what the profession does, but also on what it is. The Bar has barely been touched, and the solicitors not at all, by the student movement. Professor Twining wonders if this can last.

TWINING One of the interesting features of recent discussions of the politics of legal education is that the principal parties have been thought to be the professional bodies and the universities. There has been little mention of student power and student participation. If this comes, as seems quite likely, it is going to raise a lot of interesting questions. It will raise questions which go beyond legal education, about student participation in curriculum planning, in devising means of evaluating students, in subjects which have a professional element. One can put this in terms of a rather sneering question. 'Would you like to have your appendix taken out by a graduate of a free university?'

PLOWDEN This is not a purely academic point. Patrick Lefevre has some positive opinions on it from the Bar student's point of view.

LEFEVRE It is not since the seventeenth century that students have had even a claim to a share in government in the Inns, although we are full members of the society. Our government is controlled by Benchers, who appoint themselves – the sort of self-perpetuating wise men of the tribe. We have no say in the selection of the Benchers, nor in the control that they have over us, nor indeed in our education or indeed anything else to do with the profession. But it seems to me very important that as members of this community we ought to be given some say at least in the management of our disciplinary tribunal and in the management of our school. It is particularly important for students who are after all basically post-graduate students and students who are getting trained in the uses of administrative and other legal tribunals.

PLOWDEN In mentioning any of these doubts about current proposals, I do not mean to belittle the proposals themselves. They promise an enormous improvement on present arrangements. But underlying them all is, in various forms, an assumption which must be brought into the open if the debate is to make any sense. The assumption seems to be shared on all sides; and it is that there is a definite and distinctive role for lawyers in English society. The more conservative reformers think that if English lawyers were better educated they would be able to hold on to what they now have and, perhaps, even win back what they have lost – such as taxation work. Radical reformers think that a better educated profession could have considerably more ambitious aspirations. Michael Zander, for instance.

ZANDER It is very striking that the American lawyers dominate American society to an extent completely unknown in this country, and I think there are probably all sorts of reasons for that. One of them certainly is the fact that, as it seems to me, the American lawyers are probably the best-trained members of their society, and this is one of the reasons why they end up running, not only the legal profession, but also government, the administration, the bureaucracy, big business; wherever you look you find lawyers in charge. And I am sure that one of the reasons is that their training is more rigorous than that of other disciplines.

PLOWDEN But two things can be said about both conservative and radical views. The first is that in any social system no one sub-system – in this case the law – can be completely independent of all the others. The nature of the British political system, for instance, does not allow law and lawyers to occupy the same position in this country as they do in America. There is also the more general point that the law must largely embody the values of the society in which it operates. Some critics insist that if the law is to be regarded as a social service, especially by the less privileged sections of the community, it must be made to seem less forbidding, and less like an instrument of the ruling class. There is something in this. Michael Zander compares the reluctance of working-class clients to seek the services of a lawyer with their ready acceptance of the doctor, who is no less middle class in background. This is used as an argument for recruiting lawyers from a wider social range. But what distinguishes law from medicine is its necessary and intimate connection with social structure. As long as British social structure is such that the traditional ruling class can still command some deference, the law, to be sure of respect, must partake of the style of that class. Until the thought of a High Court judge pronouncing a life sentence in a Birmingham accent no longer seems incongruous, High Court judges must speak with the tones of Oxbridge, and so must ambitious barristers, and so must solicitors who do not wish to be thought inferior to barristers. This situation cannot be changed unilaterally by reforms in the legal profession, including changes in its members' education.

The second thing is that if lawyers are to preserve or expand their existing role, they must persuade the community that they have a distinctive and valuable contribution to make. Few people except lawyers discuss the education of lawyers; it is because of this that the assumptions underlying the discussion seem to be largely unchallenged. To go back to an earlier example, that it is a pity that the accountants and the banks have become the acknowledged experts on tax law. A pity for the lawyers, no doubt. But does it make the slightest difference to the community as a whole? Of course lawyers should know more than just the law. But there comes a point when it must be asked, to take another example, whether a certain task really calls for a lawyer who has studied social administration, rather than a social worker with a knowledge of the law.

If in future most lawyers take a law degree, and more lawyers are drawn from classes without adequate private means, the education of the profession will have to be largely supported by public money – presumably through local authority grants. Ratepayers may then want to ask some of these questions.

Perhaps it is not possible to say, in simple terms, what lawyers are *for*. Certainly I think the speakers in this programme would find it hard to agree on an answer. Professor William Twining suggests that there is no single answer, and that this makes it impossible to plan a 'rational model' for legal education.

TWINING You specify in great detail what you consider the future roles of intending lawyers to be – what skills and aptitudes and knowledge they will need to perform these roles well. You then set up a system of training to prepare them specifically to perform these tasks. The difficulty with this rational model is firstly that there is no such thing as *the* lawyer: there are many types of lawyers, and even today they are performing a very wide range of tasks. Secondly, we are living in a rapidly changing situation and formal education is a long-term investment. So one has to predict what the future roles of the lawyers will be. Thirdly, and this is perhaps the thing that gives the matter the most complexity – one does not know with regard to each particular student into what part of the system he is going to fit. One of the pressures for giving a high priority to general education is because of these difficulties of prediction. In general education, one is investing in skills, ideas and perspectives of wide application, which ought to be transferable. In a rapidly changing world the need to produce adaptable people is, I would have thought, axiomatic, because one just cannot predict what the future holds for them.

PLOWDEN This is a pretty broad conclusion. But explicitly to agree even on this would be better than simply to assume agreement on something else. It is not negative; it is just an essential first stage. Unless the Ormrod Committee, or any other body considering legal education, is prepared to question the assumptions that underlie the concept of 'the lawyer', discussion of how he should be trained will be at cross purposes, and any apparent agreement will be founded on sand.